ACKNOWLEDGEMI

CW00702579

The research for this report was funded by the and by the Community Relations Council ur Reconciliation Programme. We would particu CCRU and Mark Adair and Stella McDermott at support.

Part of this work was undertaken as part of a larger ongoing research project, funded by CCRU, into parades in Northern Ireland run by the Centre for the Study of Conflict at the University of Ulster at Coleraine. We would like to acknowledge the ongoing support and assistance of Seamus Dunn, Tom Fraser and Pat Shortt at the Centre. The Centre has published two reports on the subject of parades and the third is forthcoming. These are:

Political Rituals: Loyalist Parades in Portadown. Dominic Bryan, TG Fraser & Seamus Dunn. 1995

Parade and Protest: A Discussion of Parading Disputes in Northern Ireland. Neil Jarman & Dominic Bryan. 1996

From Riots to Rights: Nationalist Parades in the North of Ireland: Neil Jarman & Dominic Bryan. 1998

The research for this report involved travel to each of the nine countries that we discuss below. In each of those countries we received assistance from many people in a range of official, voluntary and political bodies. We do not intend to list all the people who we have interviewed and spoken to but we would give our sincere thanks to all of them and hope that we have represented their views and experiences fairly.

It is a similiar situation in Northern Ireland, where innumerable people have contributed in one form or another to our understanding this subject. However special mention must be made to Janet Quilley, Alan Quilley and Robin Wilson with whom we have had many fruitful discussions on this subject over the past two years.

We would also like to thank Colin Harper for his help and comments and James Keenan for the design and for turning the product round on an extremely tight schedule. It goes without saying that the interpretations of the material are those of the authors and responsibility for any errors remains the authors alone.

Dominic Bryan is continuing to work on the research project into issues relating to parades with the Centre for the Study of Conflict, UUC. His PhD research into the Orange Order will be published in the near future.

Nathalie Caleyron is completing a PhD from the Université de Saint Denis, Paris 8 on the influence of human rights issues on the Northern Ireland peace process.

Ciro de Rosa has a research fellowship with the Istituto Universitario Orientale in Naples. His PhD research, completed in 1997, was on the importance of symbolic practices at parades in Northern Ireland.

Neil Jarman is running a research project into political violence, community policing and public order with the Community Development Centre, North Belfast. His book Material Conflicts: Parades and Visual Displays in Northern Ireland was published by Berg in May 1997.

CONTENTS

PHOTOGRAPHS

Cover: Gay Rights activists protesting at their exclusion from the St Patrick's Day parade in New York, March 1997.

Introduction: Orangemen and RUC, Belfast June 1995.

Northern Ireland: Bandsman.

The Right to Demonstrate: Internment Rally Belfast City Hall August 1993.

England: Masquerade Performer, Notting Hill Carnival, August 1997.

Scotland: Orange Order banner at the Belfast Twelfth, July 1993.

Ireland: Dublin Fire Brigades Trade Union Pipe Band, May Day Parade, Belfast 1995.

France: Demonstrators at the International Aids Day march, Paris, December 1997.

Italy: Memorial to eight people killed by a bomb at a trade union rally in Brescia in March 1974.

USA: Uncle Sam on Parade, Boston, St Patrick's Day 1997.

Canada: Canadian Women's Orange Lodge banner.

Israel: Flags near Temple Mount, Independence Day celebrations, Jerusalem, May 1997.

South Africa: Mural depicting the march to a democratic South Africa, Cape Town, September 1997.

General Principles: Police on the Garvaghy Road, July 1997.

Appendices: Apprentice Boy, Derry Day 1992.

INTRODUCTION

Parade and Protest, published in June 1996, examined parades and demonstrations in Northern Ireland and considered possible ways of resolving or reducing disputes that had occurred over this issue. Since that time the number of disputes has risen, more areas have become involved and, after Drumcree in 1996, attitudes have become more entrenched. On the other hand, some of the changes that the report discussed have been introduced. After Drumcree 1996 the Government announced the setting up of a review into disputes over parades and marches under Sir Peter North. The Independent Review of Parades and Marches published its report in January 1997 (North Report). Its main recommendation was the setting up of a Parades Commission to facilitate mediation and to make determinations if mediation does not bring about a resolution. The Parades Commission has been in operation under the chairmanship of Alistair Graham since March 1997 but its effectiveness has been limited by the lack of statutory power. The summer of 1997 proved to be equally difficult with the dispute over the Drumcree church parade again worsening community relations. In the autumn of 1997 the Government introduced the Public Processions etc. Bill (later amended to the Public Processions Bill) which will give the Parades Commission many of the powers suggested by North.

In this report we want to further examine the way public political expression is facilitated. In particular we will compare the legislation dealing with, and the practice of managing parades and protests in Northern Ireland with that of other jurisdictions. In the first part of this report we will assess some of the changes that have taken place in Northern Ireland and examine two case studies. In the second part we will examine the legal and practical facilitation and policing of parades, demonstrations and protests in England and Wales, Scotland, the Republic of Ireland, France, Italy, the USA, Canada, Israel and South Africa. During the course of the research for this report we have visited all these countries, spoke to lawyers, police officers, civil rights & political activists and academics and visited major events such as St. Patrick's Day parades in New York and Boston and the Notting Hill Carnival in London. Quite clearly no single place is exactly comparable with Northern Ireland and it would be foolish to believe that because something works in one jurisdiction then it would work in another. Nevertheless, we believe that there are lessons in all these places that might prove instructive in developing the conditions in the north for politicians, the police and communities to start to overcome the difficulties encountered in recent years. Consequently the third part of this report brings together the variety of approaches to public political expression for comparison.

In this research we were interested in more than the formal legislative framework in which public political expression takes place. As well as examining the relevant laws in each jurisdiction, we have asked interested parties how the control of processions, carnivals, demonstrations and protests work in practice. We have asked about some of the informal mechanisms and forms of communication that have developed, and in a number of cases we have watched what has actually taken place. This report examines a number of issues that impinge upon public political expression:

- The nature of legal guarantees of the right to public political expression.
- The legal frameworks used to define and regulate the right to demonstrate and protest.
- The constraints which jurisdictions place upon public political expression
- The judgement of toleration and provocation in public political expression.
- The judgement of rights based upon tradition and custom.
- The role of the police as managers of public political expression and public order generally.
- The role of the community as managers of public political expression and public order generally.

PART ONE

Northern Ireland

The disputes over parades in 1995 raised particular issues around the rights of public political expression but 1996 crystalised those issues and forced the British Government to act. Until the stand-off at Drumcree, (Drumcree II), between 7-11 July the government had resisted calls for an inquiry into the issue of disputed parades and sustained the argument that it was a policing issue. Drumcree II saw major disturbances all over Northern Ireland, initially by loyalists whilst the parade was held from proceeding on its 'traditional' route, and later by nationalists after the police used violence to force the parade down the road. Some estimated the financial cost to be in the region of £50 million pounds and it also cost the life of a Catholic taxi driver in Lurgan shot by loyalist paramilitaries and a young man in Derry run over by a British army vehicle. On 15 July 1996 the Secretary of State Sir Patrick Mayhew announced the setting up of The Independent Review into Parades and Marches, made up of Dr Peter North (chair), Fr. Oliver Crilly and the Very Revd. John Dunlop.

Parades and Protests in 1996 and 1997

Figures produced by the RUC revealed that there were 3,161 parades in 1996, 2,405 were categorised as loyalist, 229 as republican and 527 as 'others'. Of these 8 loyalist and 11 republican parades were deemed to be illegal. As Table 1 shows there was a slight fall in numbers from the previous year, although there appears to have been an increase in the number of parades since the mid 1980s (Jarman & Bryan 1996:35-41).

Table 1

	Loyalist	Republican	Other	Total
1994	2520	272	----	2792
1995	2581 +61	302	617	3500
1996	2405 -176	229	527	3161
1997 (to 28 Sept)	2349 - 56	185	297	2831

(Source: RUC Chief Constable's Report)

The RUC figures indicate the extensive use of parades in Northern Ireland and the clear differences between communities in the organising of processions. The total also puts into perspective the number of disputes that actually take place. These statistics also indicated that in 1996 6 loyalist and 1 republican parade had conditions placed upon them whilst there was disorder at 15 loyalist parades. This compares with the previous year when there were 13 parades at which the RUC dealt with disorder, 11 loyalist and 2 republican.

Yet clearly these figures give little sense of the effect of parades disputes on community relations. The Drumcree dispute, of course, only counted as one parade in the figures. The statistics also give little indication of the chaos caused by the parades organised by the

Orange Order in the week starting Monday 8 July, in protest at the stopping of the Drumcree parade, which were clearly designed to stretch the RUC and inevitably to leave disorder in their wake, even if the parades continued down their notified route. Indeed, the organisation of the parades on a nightly basis in Belfast during that week provides a striking example of when the right to public political protest can threaten serious disruption to the life of communities (Jarman 1997).

We recorded 52 disputed parades at 22 different locations in 1996 and 59 disputed parades in 21 different locations (Tables 2 & 3 See page 25). Some of the locations that had been problematic in 1996 were not disputed in 1997, sometimes due to parades not taking place every year. Problems also developed in areas in which we are unaware of previous disputes in recent years, such as Dromore (Co. Tyrone) and Ballycastle. These statistics compare with 1995 where we calculated 41 disputes in 12 different locations.

'Croppies lie down' or Sinn Féin Conspiracy?

The preoblems over parades has been driven by the dynamic of events surrounding the disputes, by political pressure, and by the external pressures of the peace process. Contrasting experiences within the two communities can help to explain the growing intensity of the disputes. Within the nationalist community the events at Drumcree and on the Ormeau in 1996 were felt to be very important. Prior to these events, issues over rights of public political expression were important but attitudes towards the parades were still somewhat divided. Moderate nationalists and republicans were prepared to accept a degree of compromise in some areas whereby a limited number of parades could have taken place. Many nationalists felt that the RUC had taken a stand to protect their community when the Drumcree church parade was stopped in 1996. However, the RUC actions created such a reaction within the Orange Order and within loyalism generally, that the Chief Constable, Hugh Annesley, reversed his original decision and the parade was given access to the Garvaghy Road and residents forcibly removed. Later that same day the RUC judged, amid warnings that all the Orange Districts on the Belfast Twelfth parade would descend on the Ormeau Road, that the security situation was such that Ballynafeigh District should be allowed down the length of the Ormeau Road. To facilitate this they moved into the lower Ormeau area the evening before and effectively trapped residents into their streets for almost twenty-four hours. All this was done in the full glare of the world's media to allow a parade to pass at around 9.00am the following day. For many nationalists these were the clearest examples of majoritarian control of Northern Ireland since the Ulster Worker's Strike in 1974. The RUC appeared either unprepared, or unable, to stand up to intimidation from the Orange Order. Anger and disillusionment were common emotions for many at that time. Soon afterwards boycotts of Protestant owned businesses started in some areas and the bitterness was expressed in Derry when the nationalist council voted to take away the privileges of the UUP Mayor of the city Richard Dallas because he had been present at a blockade during the Drumcree stand-off. For many nationalists, the first two weeks in July 1996 were a classic case of the Orange Order wielding power to make 'the croppies lie down'.

Unionists viewed the development of these disputes quite differently. For many within the Protestant community the role of the residents groups in trying to stop loyal order parades on traditional routes has been orchestrated by Sinn Féin as an attack on Protestant culture. For those in the loyalist community the evidence was clear. A number of the residents groups had republicans or ex-prisoners as spokesperson. The demands of residents groups seemed to serve the purposes of Sinn Féin who were demanding their right to be involved in all-inclusive peace talks and the disbanding of the RUC. Finally, as 1996 progressed, it became obvious that residents groups were working more closely together. During the dispute over the Apprentice Boys' August parade the talks between the Bogside Residents Group (BRG) and Apprentice Boys' leaders seemed to hinge on the insistence by the BRG that the Apprentice Boys stop their feeder parades in other areas such as the lower Ormeau and Dunloy. For Unionists, their suspicions were confirmed when it was reported by RTE that Sinn Féin President Gerry Adams had congratulated republicans for the hard work they had done in particular areas.

Historical and Political Context

Whilst there can be no doubt that parades have always played a part in the politics of the north of Ireland, there have been various reasons for disputes developing in the mid-1990s.

- The way in which public space was controlled both before and since the partition of Ireland has meant that the Protestant community has developed a large number of 'traditional' parades whereas the Catholic community has been restricted in its political expression to predominantly Catholic areas (Jarman & Bryan 1998).
- An awareness of inequalities over public political expression became particularly significant during the period of the civil rights movement.
- The nature of the conflict since the mid-1960s has increased the sense of territoriality that many communities feel.
- The nature of the conflict since the mid-1960s has increased the assertiveness and numbers of parades and demonstrations held by Protestant and Catholic communities.
- There has long been significant resentment within the nationalist community over loyal order parades, due both to the role of the Orange Order during the Stormont era and to the perceived sectarian nature of the Orange Institution itself and elements of their public events.
- The IRA cease-fire in August 1994 allowed moderate nationalists to feel more at ease working with republicans on single-issue campaigns.
- The loyalist cease-fire allowed people to feel safer in publicly expressing political feelings in such a campaign.
- Due to concerns over the more assertive nature of some parades; due to efforts to improve community policing; and due in some measure to legal and political pressures that have been present since the mid-1980s the RUC have been less willing to facilitate loyal order parades than done in the past.
- There has been a clear change in the campaign forged by the republican movement. A greater emphasis has been place upon conducting politics in a way that develops

electoral success. The parades issue is one that allows republicans to garner broad based nationalist support by empowering local nationalist communities in a cause which highlights some fundamental problems with the RUC and exposes the unwillingness of unionists to engage in dialogue.

- Disputes prospered within an inadequate British legal and policing system in which public order appears to define what is right and what is wrong. Decisions by the police, in this case the RUC, leave everyone with the impression that 'might is right'.
  Within the above political context the parade disputes have assumed a dynamic of their
- own, with both the loyal orders and residents groups being driven by the growing symbolic importance of the issue.

In Northern Ireland parade have always tended to be a function of public order, or communal power, not of rights. Parade routes and parade 'traditions' have been dependent upon local population balance and communal deterrence, on the attitudes of the police to specific political movements, on specific legislation, and on the tolerance of communities at particular times (Jarman & Bryan 1998). This situation can only be improved if the relations between communities and the state are altered. Fundamental to this must be that rights are based upon equality, not upon the local dominance of one community over another. At issue therefore is the role that the state should play in making judgements on rights of public political expression, having regard to the fear and mistrust that exists between communities. Of vital importance is that the majority population extends the same rights to a minority community as it would claim for itself.

The North Report

The report of The Independent Review of Parades and Marches, published on 30 January 1997, made 43 main recommendations, including:

new arrangements should assist the search for accommodation and reinforce the rule of law, new arrangements should allow for the right of marchers, residents and the wider
- community to be accommodated,
  roles and responsibilities should be clarified, providing greater transparency,
- proposals should be proportionate to the problem, avoiding unnecessary restrictions and costly, bureaucratic processes,
- proposals should have the objective of achieving greater consistency in decision-making and, where practical, an accommodation in individual locations over a longer time.

The report also identified a number of principles:

- the right to peaceful free assembly should (subject to certain qualifications) be protected,

- the exercise of that right brings with it certain responsibilities; those seeking to exercise that right should take account of the likely effect on the relationships with other parts of the community and be prepared to temper their approach accordingly,

- all those involved should work towards resolution of difficulties through local accommodation,
- in the exercise of their rights and responsibilities, those involved must not condone criminal acts or offensive behaviour,
- the legislation and its application must comply with the Government's obligations under international law, and provide no encouragement for those who seek to promote disorder,
- the structure for and process of adjudication of disputes over individual parades should be clear and applied consistently with as much openness as possible,
- any procedures for handling disputes over parades and the enforcement of subsequent decisions should be proportional to the issues at stake.

The most fundamental of the proposals was to set up an independent body, which has become known as the Parades Commission, to make 'determinations' on contentious parades. However, the Chief Constable would have the power to ask the Secretary of State to review and reverse a determination. A key finding, and the one which in many ways is the hardest to interpret, is that the basis upon which decisions on parades could have conditions placed upon them would be extended to give 'consideration to the wider impact of the parade on the relationships within the community' (North 12.94). It was also recommended that the Parades Commission should issue procedures on how it might work, guidelines on the factors which would help the commissioners make these determinations and a code of conduct for those organising processions. The Parades Commission was also to facilitate mediation, work for greater understanding and arrange for monitoring of contentious parades. The North Review team felt strongly that 'rights carry responsibilities, and are not absolute', that the exercise of rights involved 'both restraint and responsibility, with respect to the well-being of others in the community' and that there was a need to work together to create a society 'that not merely tolerates but positively celebrates cultural diversity' (North 1.52).

Post-North

The reaction of residents groups to the North Report could best be described as being a cautious welcome whilst the SDLP were quick to endorse the findings. But the Report came in for immediate criticism from unionists, which described its proposals 'as a charter for grievances'. Many of the criticisms were voiced through the Northern Ireland Forum whose Standing Committee on Public Order Issues produced a report, which recommended:

- implementation of a programme explaining the culture and tradition behind traditional parades by the loyal orders;
- a code of practice based on those currently operated by the loyal order should be adopted by other organising bodies;
- that the government address flaws in the public order legislation so that the fundamental right of peaceful assembly is recognised for 'all legal organisations not supporting terrorism';

- that the RUC properly enforce provisions in legislation that make it an offence to hinder a lawful public procession;
- that traditional parades should be given particular protection.

The reaction of the Government to the North Report was to announce that although the Parades Commission would be set up, it would, in the first place, only promote and facilitate mediation and develop education around the issues of parades. Alistair Graham was appointed as Chairperson of the new Commission but the government decided on a further period of consultation before acting on the key proposals. This meant that nothing would be introduced until after the General Election which in turn meant that there was no realistic chance of a new Government introducing legislation that could have any chance of being effective for the summer of 1997. As such, the Parades Commission effectively had a watching brief over the events of the summer.

Public perception of the Parades Commission was chiefly influenced by two events during the summer. In the fall-out to the decision by the Chief Constable to forcibly remove protesters from the Garvaghy Road on 6 July a discussion document authored within the Northern Ireland Office implicated Alistair Graham in the conclusion that at least a limited parade would probably have to be allowed. Crucially this document was dated before the 'proximity talks' held by the Secretary of State at Hillsborough which members of the Garvaghy Road Residents Coalition and Armagh Orangemen attended and at which Alistair Graham was also present. Although the Parades Commission had no statutory powers and had little or no involvement in the proximity talks, and the Chief Constable made the decision under the 1987 legislation, the implication of the document was that the chairman of the Parades Commission already had a view on the Drumcree parade.

On a more positive note, the Parades Commission appeared in a more favourable light when one of its members, Revd. Roy Magee, was able assist in easing tension over parades in Newtownbutler on 12 July and attempted to find agreement on two Black parades in August. However, despite continued attempts, a church parade on 3 August ended in disturbances when the RUC permitted the parade to take place, although the Black Preceptory voluntarily re-routed their parade on 9 August (Kelly & Allen Nan 1998). The involvement of Magee raised an important issue over the role of the Parades Commission. Could Commissioners be involved in mediation if legislation was also to give them powers to make determinations as well? The possible conflict between the two roles led Roy Magee to resign from the Commission late in 1997. It remains to be seen what the public expectation will be over the role the Commission might play in the coming year.

The Public Processions Bill

The new Labour Government published The Public Processions Etc. (Northern Ireland) Bill in October 1997. Whilst its main aim was to empower the Parades Commission, publicity mainly focused on the clause which allowed for the remit to be widened to consider expressions of cultural identity other than parades. This clause was apparently put in at the request of Orangemen during negotiations over the Twelfth parades that were eventually voluntarily re-routed in the summer. However, as the Bill passed through Parliament it seemed to become obvious that expressions of cultural identity might include such things as the painting of kerbstones and the flying of flags. If as unionists claimed the Parades Commission is to be a factory of grievances, then the clause on other forms of cultural expression simply increased the size of the factory! The clause was dropped and the bill renamed The Public Processions (Northern Ireland) Bill.

At the same time the Parades Commission published three documents for consultation: a Code of Conduct, giving guidance to those in processions, Procedural Rules by which the practices of the Commission will be regulated and Guidelines setting the basis on which the determinations will be made (see Appendix for an overview of the Public Processions Bill, Code of Conduct, Procedural Rules and Guidelines).

Three issues in the Bill and associated documents are of particular importance. First, the criteria on which the Commission are to make the decision; second, the role of the police in the process; and third the publication by the Parades Commission of a 'preliminary view' on parades in areas of dispute.

The Criteria for Determinations

Clause 7 (6) sets out the basis on which the Commission should make a determination:

...the Commission shall have regard to -
(a) any public disorder or damage to property which may result from the procession;
(b) any disruption to the life of the community which the procession may cause;
(c) any impact which the procession may have on relationships within the community
(d) any failure of a person of any description specified in the guidelines to comply with the Code of Conduct (whether in relation to the procession in question or any previous procession); and
(e) the desirability of allowing a procession customarily held along a particular route to be held along that route.

A number of points arise from these criteria:
- How does one measure the various criteria against each other?
- On what basis is the Parades Commission to make judgements of public disorder?
- How does one measure 'disruption to the life of the community' or 'the impact a procession may have on relationships within the community'?
- Who will monitor compliance to the Code of Conduct?
- Why should a traditional route carry precedence over others and on what basis do you measure tradition?

The Role of the RUC

There are serious issues about the RUC that impinge upon this debate but which have been considered in more detail by others (Bryett 1997; CAJ 1996, 1997; Human Rights Watch 1997; O'Rawe & Moore 1998). However, concentrating on the parading legislation there are questions over the exact role of the Chief Constable in carrying out the determinations. It is broadly accepted that a police force has to have operational control on managing a large event; public safety demands that officers may be required to change decisions. However, the Public Processions legislation allows for more than this. The Chief Constable can appeal to the Secretary of State to review a determination of the Parades Commission. The Committee for the Administration of Justice has argued that there is no reason for the police having a 'double bite of the cherry' by making an appeal, given that the Chief Constable will already have made representations to the Commission. Furthermore the Chief Constable is not accountable to the Parades Commission if he feels the need to overturn their determination.

The Preliminary View

The explanatory note that accompanies the new legislation suggests that the Public Processions Bill 'implements recommendations contained in the Report of the Independent Review of Parades and Marches'. In some areas, such as the clause on traditionality, the legislation is clearly at variance with North (see North 12.53). However, one proposal has caused particular difficulties. North recommended that 'the Parades Commission should be empowered to reach and promulgate conclusions to one or more parades in an area and do so where appropriate over a period longer than one year'. One advantage of this is that each determination is not reduced to a win-lose scenario. Considering more than one parade over a particular time frame however is problematic since under the new legislation notification of intent to parade is to be made 28 days in advance. Each parade can therefore only be considered on its own merits. Yet it is recognised that the number of parades in a particular area influences community relations. As such, under the Parade Commission's Procedural Rules, having gathered information in particular areas, the Commission will make an early informal or preliminary view on the pattern of parades for the year ahead. This offers a possible blueprint on the marching season and may receive cross-community support. The most significant change from previous years may well be that there will now be a preliminary view made on the right to march a particular route, which is distanced from any impending threat of public disorder.

Practice

So far we have concentrated on changes made by the state on the procedures for deciding on the right to march. However, just as important is an analysis of how the control of public political expression works in practice. A number of issues merit consideration:

- the responsibility of organisers;
- the role of the community in controlling public order;
- the stewarding of events;
- police responses to public order situations;

- levels of toleration and provocation;
- the consumption of alcohol.

Let us take two examples to consider how these issues affect practical situations.

Case Study One: Apprentice Boys Parade - Ormeau Road 8 April 1996

The annual Apprentice Boys Easter Monday parade was held in Portadown in 1996. The Walker Club in Ballynafeigh customarily holds a feeder parade that starts at the Orange Hall near the top of the road and finishes by boarding buses near the city centre. Tension was still high in the lower Ormeau area after violence during the RUC's clearance of protesters to allow the Apprentice Boys to hold a procession the previous August, and the Lower Ormeau Concerned Community (LOCC) group gave notice of a protest. The RUC announced that the Apprentice Boys parade would be re-routed.

At 8.00am around 80 men left the Orange Hall with approximately 50 more people following on the pavement. A banner at the front of the parade stated 'Ballynafeigh says No to Re-routing'. The RUC had blocked the bridge using Land Rovers, but officers were not at this point dressed in riot gear. Sandy Geddis, who acted as spokesman for the club, read a statement at the RUC line and the marchers stood around chatting. Things remained quiet until 9.30 when the RUC pushed through lines of Apprentice Boys to give a fire engine access to a fire that had been started at the rear of the nearby supermarket. As the accompanying media scrambled to get pictures there were scuffles, a cameraman's step-ladder was thrown into the river, and the reporters retreated behind police lines. It became clear that the parade organisers were not sure how they were going to conduct the stand-off.

It was a warm, sunny day and many people sat around drinking. There was some intermittent bottle but during the afternoon the violence became more persistent and a number of people were injured, apparently from bottles falling short of police lines. The police seemed to assume that the Apprentice Boys would march back to the hall at 5.00pm when the original parade would have returned from Portadown. However, the Apprentice Boys did not seem to have a clear idea of how they were going to end the protest and the majority of those confronting police lines were not wearing Apprentice Boys sashes. From 4.00pm onwards a number of bands arrived and marched down to the police lines. Some Apprentice Boys and band members were clearly ill at ease at how the protest was being conducted and two band members had a public argument about what was taking place.

The next phase saw petrol bombs being prepared and we believe there may have been an attempt to hijack a bus. Some shops were attacked whilst others in the crowd shouted at people 'not to attack our own'. Between 5.00 and 6.00pm, perhaps when it became obvious to the police that the Apprentice Boys were not going to parade back, the riot squad began to advance up the road. At around 6.30 there were attempts by some older men to gain control of the situation. One accordion band marched down to police lines then back up the road, which changed the mood somewhat and switched attention from police lines. Another band also marched to the police lines, but by this time significant figures had taken control at the front of the crowd and this allowed Unionist councillors and some Apprentice Boys to place themselves between the crowd and the police and relieve tensions.

Just when the situation appeared to be under control another band and an Apprentice Boys club appeared at the top of the road and marched down. As the band moved away some of these Apprentice Boys attacked the police with a bannerette and ceremonial pike whilst others attempt to pull them back and retain control. After further confrontations those in the crowd trying to maintain control manage to do so. It was only at about 11.00 at night that the police broke up the remaining crowd with a baton charge.

Observations

The events that took place during the day were complex. There were clearly interactions between the apparent randomness of crowd activity and the involvement of a variety of interest groups. There was the Apprentice Boys club, a variety of bands from different parts of the city, some with paramilitary affiliations, some without, there was a variety of unionist politicians, there were figures from both the UDA and UVF present, many spectators spent the time drinking. The actions of the police were crucial and the role of the media was significant on at least one occasion. At different points during the day different elements in the crowd took centre stage and seemed to control what was taking place.

However it would be foolish to think that situations such as these can always be managed. Emotions were high, yet there was clearly a desire amongst the organisers of the parade, amongst many unionist politicians and, we suspect, amongst some within the paramilitaries, to control what was taking place and make the protest forceful yet peaceful. The protest therefore raises a number of questions.

- Is it possible to plan protests in such a way as to keep the peace?
- Could organisers utilise stewards to manage such situation better?
- Can communication with the police be improved so misunderstandings do not occur?
- With whom does the responsibility for public order lie, the police or the protesters?
- Can effective controls on alcohol consumption be maintained in such circumstances?
- Should the media be working under guidelines for such occasions?

Case Study Two: Parades in Derry

The parade dispute in Derry has some features that are significantly different from those in other areas (Jarman & Bryan 1996; Pat Finucane Centre 1995 & 1996; Kelly & Allen Nan 1998). First it is a city with a large nationalist community with a small Protestant community in the Fountain area. There seems to be widespread agreement that it is important that the city remains mixed and that the Protestant legacy is recognised. Second, the dispute involves a small number of parades: the Apprentice Boys parade in August commemorating the end of the Siege and the parade in December which remembers the Closing of the Gates and ends with the burning of an effigy of Lundy. The August parade is possibly the largest parade held annually by the loyal orders. Third, there seems to be a consensus in the city that these two parades should take place, but there are disagreements about the conditions under which the parade should take place.

In 1995 the Apprentice Boys applied to have a parade around the full circuit of the walls of Derry on the morning of Saturday 12 August. The walls had been closed in 1969 so the full circuit had not been walked since then. The Bogside Residents Group (BRG), formed in 1995, objected to the parade using the section walls overlooking the Bogside. However, the police decided the parade should go ahead and cleared protesters from the wall. Later in the day when the main parade came over from the Waterside there were confrontations, particularly between some bandsmen and protesters at the Diamond. Although Apprentice Boys stewards attempted to calm the situation, they were unable to deal with it. After the parade ended conflict developed between the police and protesters and within 30 minutes plastic bullets were being fired and petrol bombs being thrown.

The events surrounding Drumcree 1996 encouraged a closer relationship between the various residents groups and members of the BRG felt that they should show solidarity with residents groups in areas where the Catholic community formed a lower percentage of the community. During meetings between the BRG and the Apprentice Boys prior to the 1996 Relief of Derry parade, the BRG argued that a solution should be linked to disputed Apprentice Boys parades in the lower Ormeau, Bellaghy, and Dunloy. But with no agreement reached the Secretary of State, Sir Patrick Mayhew, decided to prohibit all parades on that section of the city walls between 7 - 31 August and the army moved in and sealed the area. The parade on the day took place without major incidents, thanks in part to Alistair Simpson, Governor of the Apprentice Boys announcing that a parade around the walls would take place at a date of their choosing. That parade took place on 19 October.

In 1997 there were significant attempts by community workers, politicians, the business community, the BRG and the Apprentice Boys to look for solutions. Yet, as with the previous year, the feeder parades in other areas still created difficulties. On 4 August the RUC announced that the controversial feeder parades were to be re-routed and the BRG announced that there would be no protest at the Siege of Derry parade. There seemed to be a good chance that the day would pass peacefully. As part of an effort to change the atmosphere at the parades around the walls, the Apprentice Boys organised a pageant, which was in part funded by Derry City Council. Alistair Simpson made it clear that only local club members were to take part, and although there was a group of around 30 nationalists on Magazine Street, at 9.30 the parade, with some people in costume, took place to the sound of a single drum beat. Whilst members of the local Apprentice Boys Clubs went to the Cathedral for services other people were left drinking, waiting for the main parade. This started from the Waterside around mid-day and included nearly 150 bands. Although there was no organised protest in the centre of Derry, there were clearly a number of onlookers from the Bogside gathered in Butchers Street. The police attempted to let spectators move freely around the Diamond although there were barriers in place. For a long period the parade seemed likely to pass off peacefully but a number of factors conspired to cause disturbances. As is always the case there are significant quantities of drink taken by spectators at this event and some were allowed to occupy the War Memorial. Young nationalists were soon engaging in 'banter'. Although there were attempts to keep the situation calm, things rapidly got out of control when a loyalist band, carrying paramilitary flags, broke ranks to pursue a youngster who had stolen a bandsman's cap. Members of the band gestured as if they were shooting at people as stewards and police struggled to regain control. For the next hour tension was high, bottles were thrown, and fights broke out. Apprentice Boys stewards tried in vain to calm the situation but as more loyalists gathered in Bishop Street, confrontation became inevitable. As bands came into the Diamond a number of them reacted, ignoring the fact that they were going around a war memorial. Since the RUC seemed unwilling to deal with the parade they tended to move in on the nationalists. Only when the parade had finished did the RUC move against the loyalists who had gathered and the riot squad moved them up Bishop Street.

These incidents soured the genuine efforts to improve the environment in which the parade took place. The Apprentice Boys were quick to act against the band involved, but recriminations over the action of organisers, police and those watching the parade were widespread. The Closing of the Gates parade on 13 December subsequently became an issue even though it had not been so in previous years. The BRG stated that they would protest in the Diamond. Interestingly, the business community, who had been trying to resolve problems, now moved to centre stage and debate focused on the way the parade affected the Christmas trade. Attempts to find a resolution failed and on the day the police put in place a massive operation to stop protesters reaching the Diamond. Whilst businesses in the Bishop Street area had felt it necessary to close in previous years the threat of disturbances and the police operation effectively meant that most of the city centre closed down by early afternoon.

The parade is much smaller than that in August and involves around twelve bands. It comes into the city around mid-day and, after a service at the Cathedral, follows a route around the Diamond. Whilst there was shouting between protesters and loyalists on the ground the atmosphere was not particularly bad. The police operation overwhelmed almost everyone including parade organisers. A helicopter flew so low overhead that it was not easy to hear anything. Apprentice Boys stewards made strenuous efforts to make sure that there were no problems as the bands went around the Diamond. Some paramilitary flags that had been on view as the parade entered the city were removed and stewards attempted to keep spectators from abusing the protesters. Senior Apprentice Boys were placed in Butchers Street where the parade enters the Diamond and made sure that each band knew to stop playing. Indeed, the first band set the mood by playing Jingle Bells as they approached. The parade went smoothly until a Belfast band changed the atmosphere despite attempts by stewards to calm them down. As they went around the Diamond a confrontation with a steward required police involvement and brief scuffles resulted. Following the parade confrontations between police and nationalists quickly developed on Shipquay Street, these spread to the bus station and the Guildhall area. Vehicles were hijacked and burnt as youngsters threw stones and petrol bombs at the police. Serious confrontations continued late into the evening.

Observations

Unlike most loyal order parades, the majority of those participating in the Siege of Derry parade are not from the area and are relatively unfamiliar with the city. Since there is a large Catholic majority in the city many locals feel that their city is taken over for the day. This in turn increases the problems for those trying to steward the event if an incident occurs. For many it is a day out and there are often problems with the amount of drinking that takes place at both the August and December parades. The parades also take the best part of both days. The December event has particular problems because the effigy of Lundy is not burnt until after dark so that many people are hanging around for most of the afternoon.

Coming to terms with the historical legacy provided by the two major events is important for the future of the city. It is important for all concerned that the Protestant community in the city feels secure and that Derry is able to accommodate its diverse history. However, for this to take place the relations that encompass the parades need to be worked upon. Although 1997 was an inauspicious year for improving the community relations in the city there is clearly a lot of pressure to make things work. The business community and the local council have been more pro-active in Derry than in any other part of Northern Ireland. The Apprentice Boys have approached the situation with more imagination than the loyal orders have shown in other areas and the BRG have repeatedly said that in the right conditions these parades should be facilitated. Neither the business community, nor local residents, nor the Apprentice Boys can reasonably claim (or we think would try to claim) a monopoly of rights in using the city centre. The disputes in Derry also raise a range of issues.

- What level of disruption should reasonably be asked of local communities in recognising the right of groups to hold public events?
- How much should one take into account the rights of the business community in decisions on major events?
- How can changes to the organisation of events improve local community relations?
- What levels of police-organiser-community liaison should there be prior to large public events?
- Is it possible to improve the monitoring and stewarding of such events to better ensure public order?
- Can improved communications better facilitate public order?
- What strategies can be utlised to reduce the amount of incidents exacerbated by the high consumption of alcohol at events?

Conclusions

These two case studies provide good examples of the complex issues we wish to analyse. In some ways they are not representative cases. The Apprentice Boys of Derry have many any fewer parades than the Orange Order and as an organisation have attempted to deal with some of these difficult issues on the Ormeau Road and in Derry. The attempt to view the walk on the walls as an historical pageant must surely be a good way of coming to terms with difficult relationships. Nevertheless, despite the unique qualities of these cases we do think they suggest general problems.

The Right to Parade

The right to hold a procession or demonstration is an important right and it is the duty of the state to attempt to facilitate that right. But where do the limits of these rights lie?

> What are the responsibilities of organisers?
> What constraints should be placed on those wanting to hold processions?
> What are the limits of provocation that either participants or protesters should tolerate?
> What rights should be accorded to the business community?
> How do we judge that groups are being treated equally?

The Right to Protest

The right to protest is important and it is the duty of the police to facilitate that right. Clearly, in the nature of protests, they offer different problems to events such as a parade.

> What responsibility do those protesting have towards the community?
> How are relations with the police to be managed?
> Is it possible to lay out guidelines for protests?
> Does a democratic culture require greater education on rights?

Policing

One conclusion that can be drawn is that public order is an issue for the wider community not simply for the police. Serious and regular breakdowns in public order generally affect areas that can least afford such problems. Recognising that public order is a problem for the community is not new and it has led to a reappraisal of policing in other parts of the world, South Africa being an obvious example (Brogden & Shearing 1993). Such problems therefore demand a re-examination of the advantages of forms of local community empowerment and a rethinking of the way we deal with public order problems.

In the second section of this report we will examine how many of the above issues are addressed in other countries. The Notting Hill Carnival, the control of Orange parades in Scotland, the legal rights of demonstrators in France and Italy, the reform of rights of political assembly and the management of political difference in South Africa, the control of large St Patrick's Day parades in New York and Boston, and the rights of minority communities in Israel are all worthy of examination. Many similar legal and practical problems exist in each of these jurisdictions. Whilst in some cases people have had no more success in dealing with problems than in Northern Ireland, we think that they offer a range of possibilities and solutions which are worth considering.

TABLE 2   PARADE DISPUTES IN 1996

Mar	3	Lurgan	Nationalist Right to March	Re-route
April	8	Ormeau Road	ABs - Feeder Parade	Re-route/Violence
	20	Crossgar	Band Parade	Violence
	26	Lurgan	Band Parade	Voluntary re-route/Protest
	28	Ormeau Road	OO - Orange Widows Service	Re-route
May	4	Lurgan	Band Parade	Voluntary re-route/Protest
	5	West Belfast	Hunger Strikes Commemoration	Voluntary re-route
	19	Dunloy	ABs - Church Parade	Protest
	31	Roslea	Black Banner Unfurling	Protest
June	9	Dunloy	Black Church Parade	Protest
	21	North Belfast	OO mini-12th - Tour of the North	Protest/Violence
	29	West Belfast	OO mini-12th - Whiterock	Protest
		Downpatrick	Band Parade	Re-route
	30	Ormeau Road	OO - Somme Anniversary	Re-route
July	1	Lurgan	OO - Somme Commemoration	Protest
		Bellaghy	OO - Somme Commemoration	Protest
	7	Portadown	OO - Drumcree Church Parade	Re-route/Violence
	8	Bellaghy	Band Parade	Protest
	12	Ormeau Road	OO - Twelfth Feeder	Protest
		Newry	OO - Twelfth Feeder	Protest-re-route
		Coalisland	OO - Twelfth Feeder	Protest/re-route
		Keady	OO - Twelfth Feeder	Protest
		Newtownbutler	OO - Twelfth Feeder	Protest
		Pomeroy	OO - Twelfth Feeder	Protest
	19	Omagh	Band and Nationalist Parades	Violence
	21	Newtownbutler	Black Church Parade	Protest/re-route
	27	Keady	Band Parade	Protest/Violence
Aug	10	Derry	ABs - Relief of Derry	Re-route
		Armagh	ABs - Feeder	Protest/re-route
		Bellaghy	ABs - Feeder	Protest
		Dunloy	ABs - Feeder	Re-route
		Ormeau Road	ABs - Feeder	Re-route
		Newtownbutler	Black - Feeder	Protest/ re-route
		Roslea	Black - Feeder	Protest/re-route
	11	Bellaghy	Black Church Parade	Protest/re-route
	15	Moy	AOH Lady Day Parade	Voluntary re-route
	25	Ormeau Road	Black Church Parade	Voluntary re-route
	30	Crumlin	Band Parade	Violence
		Newry	Band Parade	Protest/re-route
	31	Armagh	Black - Feeder	Protest/re-route
		Bellaghy	Black - Feeder	Protest/re-route
		Cookstown	Black - Feeder	Protest

		Crumlin	Black - Feeder	Protest/re-route
		Dunloy	Black - Feeder	Protest/re-route
		Keady	Black - Feeder	Voluntary re-route
		Newry	Black - Feeder	Protest/re-route
		Ormeau Road	Black - Feeder	Protest/re-route
		Pomeroy	Black - Feeder	Protest/re-route
		Strabane	Black - Feeder	Protest/re-route
Sep	7	Derry	Women's Orange Parade	Attacked
	8	Dunloy	OO - Church Parade	Protest/re-route
	22	Enniskillen	Band Parade	Violence
Oct	27	Ormeau	OO - Church Parade	Re-route

TABLE 3   PARADE DISPUTES 1997

Mar 31	Ormeau Road	ABs - Feeder	Voluntary re-route
April 27	Ormeau Road	OO - Orange Widows Service	Voluntary re-route
May 18	Dunloy	ABs Church Parade	Protest/re-route
June 7	Ballymena	Band Parade	Violence
20	Newry	Band Parade	Protest
22	Bellaghy	OO - Church Parade	Protest/re-route
	Keady	OO - Church Parade	Protest/re-route
	Mountfield	OO - Church Parade	Protest/re-route
28	West Belfast	OO mini 12th - Whiterock	Protest
29	Ormeau Road	OO - Somme Anniversary	Re-route
July 1	Bellaghy	Somme Anniversary	Protest/re-route
4	Newtownbutler	Church - Band Parade	Voluntary re-rout
6	Keady	OO - Church Parade	Voluntary re-route
	Newtownbutler	OO- Church Parade	Protest/Voluntary re-route
	Pomeroy	OO - Church Parade	Protest
	Portadown	OO - Drumcree Church parade	Protest
7	Bellaghy	Band Parade	Protest/re-route
12	Armagh	OO - Twelfth Main	Voluntary re-route
	Ballycastle	IOO - Twelfth Main	Protest
	Bellaghy	OO - Twelfth Feeder	Protest/re-route
	Castlewellan	OO - Twelfth Feeder	Protest/re-route
	Derry	OO - Twelfth Main	Protest/Voluntary re-route
	Dromore	OO - Twelfth Main	Agreement
	Dunloy	OO - Twelfth Feeder	Protest/re-route
	Keady	OO - Twelfth Feeder	Protest/Voluntary re-route
	Newry	OO - Twelfth Feeder	Voluntary re-route
	Newtownbutler	OO - Twelfth Feeder	Agreement
	Ormeau Road	OO - Twelfth Feeder	Voluntary re-route
	Pomeroy	OO - Twelfth Feeder	Protest
	Strabane	OO - Twelfth Feeder	Protest/Voluntary re-route
	Whitewell Rd	OO - Twelfth Feeder	Voluntary re-route
14	Newry	Black - Feeder	Voluntary re-route
25	Castlewellan	Band Parade	Agreement
26	Ormeau Road	Band Parade	Violence
Aug 3	Newtownbutler	Black Church Parade	Protest
8	Ballycastle	Band Parade	Violence
9	Bellaghy	ABs - Feeder	Protest/re-route
	Derry	ABs - Main	Agreement/Violence
	Dunloy	ABs - Feeder	Re-route
	Newtownbutler	Black - Feeder	Protest
	Ormeau Road	ABs - Feeder	Re-route
	Roslea	Black - Feeder	Re-route

	24	Ormeau Road	Black - Church Parade	Voluntary re-route
	29	Newry	Band Parade	Protest
		Pomeroy	Band Parade	Protest
	30	Ballycastle	Black - Feeder	Protest
		Bellaghy	Black - Feeder	Re-route
		Dunloy	Black - Feeder	Voluntary re-route
		Newry	Black - Feeder	Voluntary re-route
		Ormeau Road	Black - Feeder	Voluntary re-route
		Pomeroy	Black - Feeder	Voluntary re-route
		Strabane	Black - Feeder	Voluntary re-route
		Whitewell Rd	Black - Feeder	Voluntary re-route
	31	Lurgan	Another Chance	Protest
Sep	5	Crumlin	Band Parade	Protest
	14	Dunloy	OO - Church parade	Re-route
Oct	26	Ormeau Road	OO - Church parade	Re-route
Nov	8	Bellaghy	British Legion - Rem Sun	Protest
Dec	13	Derry	ABs	Violence

PART TWO

The Right to Demonstrate
Case Studies of Law and Practice

Freedom of assembly and the right to demonstrate and to protest are widely accepted as basic civil rights and as such are embodied within all international charters of human rights. However, notwithstanding the universality of the principle, the various charters always allow for local interpretation of such ideals and therefore each legal jurisdiction has power to place limits on this and other rights.

The case studies that we present in the following sections are drawn from a diverse range of countries. Each of these countries acknowledges, either through adopting international human rights charters, by constitutional guarantees, by legal articles, by common law or by a combination of these, the importance of freedom of assembly and the right to demonstrate. But many of these countries have also encountered a variety of problems over the practical expression of these basic rights and each country has developed its own means of balancing generalised ideals with local context. The value of presenting such case studies lies in the way that they can illustrate the wider context within which the laws and constitutional rights are interpreted in practice.

What becomes clear from these examples is that there is no single model that can be held up as the perfect balance of ideal and practice. Each country will always have to balance an idealised concept of rights with local context. Nevertheless there is a limited range of issues that continue to be addressed when dealing with this subject. Sometimes these can be dealt with by law or through the courts, sometimes they have to be dealt with in a more fluid and pragmatic way, by developing good practice over time.

Good practice cannot be imposed. It evolves over a period of time at the interface of power relations between civil society and the state, between groups who wish to demonstrate, groups who wish to protest and those who have responsibility for the control of public order. This evolution will not necessarily be entirely harmonious or peaceful. The interests of the state and the interests of the various sections of civil society will not always coincide, anymore than civil society could be seen as a unified or homogenous body with only one set of interests.

The case studies show that parades, demonstrations, protests and marches are a fundamental part of the democratic process. They are also almost inevitability a source of conflict. To protest or demonstrate in favour of something means to protest or demonstrate against something else. Most protesting will offend somebody. In fact one could go so far as to say that if something is worth protesting about it ought to offend somebody.

If the parties involved are not willing to compromise and recognise the complexity involved in balancing the multiplicity of rights and responsibilities it is difficult, if not impossible, to impose a lasting solution on social conflict. Some form of order might be imposed through regulation, but may merely become a target in itself. If this new order is successfully destroyed, then one has 'proved' that it was not a fair compromise.

Conflicts and disputes can be used to restrict the rights both of individuals and of communities, but they can also be used to consolidate, to extend and to clarify civil rights.

While rights might be, or might seem to be, restricted during disputes, the process of resolving conflict should be part of the process of debating the nature of human rights and civil rights, their role in a democratic society, how they are balanced with social responsibilities and how they are to be safeguarded.

These case studies show that the disputes over the right to parade in Northern Ireland are not unique, similar problems have arisen in many of the countries that we have studied. We also hope that these examples illustrate that there is a wide range of ways through which such problems can be addressed and some of them may be appropriate in Northern Ireland.

To repeat a point made earlier, there is no single or correct way to deal with the problem of balancing rights and responsibilities. But finding a solution does require a willingness from all parties involved to compromise and to negotiate, and a genuine desire to seek a resolution.

England & Wales

Many of the issues that surround the right to hold parades in Northern Ireland have also, in some form or another, been raised in Britain, and the legislation pertaining to marches has much in common with that in England and Wales and in Scotland. Unlike many countries the right to public political activity is not enshrined within a Bill of Rights, rather it is based on common law. That is, civil rights are 'protected by the principle that people have the right to do anything which is not expressly forbidden by law' (Hadden & Donnelly 1997:16). Yet in practice, as the right to march and demonstrate is not enshrined in a Bill of Rights, there have always been reasons that the authorities could use to prevent meetings or processions, and during the twentieth century various pieces of public order legislation have effectively superseded common law (Card 1987: 57-80; North 1997:89-107).

Legislation

Public order legislation giving the police powers to restrict processions was first introduced in 1936, in large part to deal with the fascist movement in England. At the time this was opposed by civil libertarians as being profoundly 'un-British' (Townshend 1993:104-111). One of the ways that the 1936 Act tried to deal with fascism and the development of private armies was to restrict the wearing of uniforms. This had of course long been common practice in Ireland and had given particular concern to the British authorities between 1912 and 1914 with the development of the Ulster Volunteer Force. However many who wore a uniform would have been considered harmless and as such, legislation was difficult to introduce and even harder to enforce. Whilst the issues of the wearing of uniforms did not trouble the state in the long run, the right to hold meetings and processions had become governed by public order legislation and the police gained formal powers to impose conditions on events.

The policing of public political events was not without problems in the post-war period, particularly in the 1970s when anxieties were raised during the miners' strikes and demonstrations involving the National Front. But it was only in the 1980s as a result of the rioting in areas such as Brixton, Southall and Toxteth and the 1984 NUM strike that public order became a high profile issue. Policing practice was analysed, developed and influenced particularly by reports produced by Lord Scarman on disturbances both in Northern Ireland and Britain and new legislation was introduced in 1986. In his report after the riots in Brixton in 1981 Scarman had argued that:

> A balance has to be struck, a compromise found that will accommodate the exercise of the right to protest within a framework of public order which enables ordinary citizens, who are not protesting, to go about their business and pleasure without obstruction or inconvenience. The fact that those who are at any time concerned to secure the tranquillity of the streets are likely to be the majority must not lead us to deny the protesters their right to march; the fact that the protesters are desperately sincere and are exercising a fundamental human right must not lead us to overlook the rights of the majority. (Lord Scarman 1981 quoted Townshend 1993:149)

The Scarman Report acknowledged that public order policing in Britain relied on a society in which there was some considerable degree of consensus (Townshend 1993:159-166). In the 1970s and 1980s such a consensus had become increasingly difficult to find. The Public Order Act 1986 increased police powers in a way that some have argued detracts from individual civil liberties (Card 1987:6). The Act requires organisers to give advance notice of a parade to the police, although many local authorities had previously required such notice and many organisers would have freely provided it. There is an exemption 'where the procession is one commonly or customarily held in the police area (or areas) in which it is proposed to be held' although there is no clear definition of what 'commonly or customarily held' means. One should note that while this differed from legal provisions in Northern Ireland, where it is the customarily held route that is specified, it might well apply to events such as Orange parades in Liverpool.

The Act also allows for the Chief Constable to impose conditions upon a procession prior to an event or a senior police officer who is present at the procession. Conditions can be imposed on the grounds of the possibility of serious public disorder, serious damage to property or 'serious disruption to the life of the community' or if the Chief Constable believes 'the purpose, whether express or not, of the persons organising it is the intimidation of others with a view to compelling them not to do an act they have a right to do, or to do an act they have a right not to do' (S.12.1). This last criteria effectively tries to differentiate intimidation from persuasion although as we are well aware in Northern Ireland making judgements on what constitutes intimidation is not always easy.

A ban on a parade can only be imposed if serious public disorder is likely and the police have insufficient powers to impose conditions to prevent the disorder. The Chief Constable has to make an application to ban processions, or a class of procession (it is not possible to ban a single procession), to the local council or borough who may approve such an order with the consent of the Home Secretary. In London, where events tend to have more national rather than local significance, the district councils are not involved and the Commissioner of the City of London Police or the Metropolitan Police can make a banning order with the consent of the Home Secretary. Note also that it is not possible for local residents or a local authority to force a Chief Constable to impose conditions as was attempted by Lewisham Borough Council under the old legislation over a National Front march in April 1980 (Card 1987:88-92).

Public assemblies do not carry the same legal restrictions as processions and no form of notice is required to hold a public meeting. Card argues that in some senses this is anomalous since protest meetings can be just as likely to cause public disorder as a procession. But the 1985 Government white paper, Review of Public Order Law, argued that it would be too substantial a restriction of freedom (meetings and assemblies apparently being deemed more important than marches) and that the administrative burden would be too great (Card 1987:82). However conditions can be imposed on assemblies by a senior police officer on the same grounds as those for a procession.

As has happened in Northern Ireland in recent years, conditions or bans imposed on processions can be taken to judicial review. However, it must be remembered that in the main a judicial review does not examine the merits of a case but simply checks that correct procedures have been followed in reaching the original decision

The Notting Hill Carnival

The Carnival held in the Notting Hill area of London over the August bank holiday weekend involves an estimated million and a half people and is one of the largest annual public events to be held in Britain. It is the largest single routine policing operation and in the early 1990s required 9,000 officers, with costs estimated at £3 million (Waddington 1994:18). It is a complex event involving a moving parade of floats and masquerade dancers that travels a three-mile route and a number of stationary sound systems. It is highly diverse event that increasingly involves not only the ethnic Caribbean communities but also reflects the cosmopolitan, international, nature of London; Carnival draws thousands of spectators from Europe and other parts of the world.

Whilst the Notting Hill Carnival has developed its own specific localised cultural forms it shares characteristics with many other similar events around the world. It is a heady pleasurable mixture of masking, anonymity, fantasy, sexuality, alcohol and other drugs. An opportunity for individuals to express themselves in ways they would feel unable to do at any other time. It provides an occasion when social norms are abandoned or inverted. It provides a time when some of the structures of power of the society are temporarily excluded from an area, where people masked by costume can both act anonymously and be on centre stage within a large crowd. For many participants who are allowed to dance the streets to their own rhythms it is a deeply empowering event (Alleyne-Dettmers 1996).

The Development of Carnival

Carnival as a general cultural form has been around for hundreds of years and has developed in a range of historical and geographical contexts. The roots of the Notting Hill Carnival can be found in Trinidad where West African slaves celebrated emancipation in 1834 by drawing on European festival and African cultural forms in public expression. Carnival provided opportunities to show political opposition and to express a public identity within the complexities of Trinidadian society (Alleyne-Dettmers 1996, van Koningsbruggen 1997).

The development of a Carnival in Notting Hill stems from the influx of West Indians into the Ladbroke Grove area of west London. The area had seen race riots in 1958 and suffered growing social problems in the years that followed. There is some dispute about when and how the Carnival was started (Cohen 1993; Wills 1996), but in 1966 a multi-ethnic fair took place which over the years came to increasingly take the form of a Carnival. In 1968 the lack of support from the Royal Borough of Kensington and Chelsea and local business led to the event being dubbed the 'Carnival of the poor'. In the 1970s racial tension increased and relations between the police and the local black community worsened,particularly with the random use of stop and search tactics on black youths. Carnival took on more West Indian cultural forms first through Trinidadian steel bands and masquerading and then later in the decade with Jamaican Rastafarianism and reggae sound systems. In 1975 attendance reached a quarter of a million and a significant increase in crime was reported. The following year 1,500 police officers were used and they apparently acted in a high handed way, confrontations between youths and police developed and hundreds of people were injured. The violence further fractured relationships between the police and organisers but also revealed the stresses between the Trinidadian style Carnival and the more overtly politicised Jamaican Rastafarianism. The disturbances of 1976 also convinced the Metropolitan police to equip themselves with reinforced plastic riot shields (Waddington 1994:19).

Relations between the police and black youths remained poor for much of the 1980s, fuelled by continuing use of stop and search tactics by the police and raids on local social centres. Each year Carnival proved a potential focus for political confrontation as well as an arena for crime. The authorities felt duty bound to provide massive policing, while the organisers regularly asked the police not to provoke the youth by appearing in large numbers. Yet whilst the organisers complained at the high profile police presence they had failed to take responsibility for maintaining order themselves. In 1977 they had hired hundreds of stewards but these were quickly over run by youths, many stewards took off their T-shirts and disappeared into the crowds. Over the years there have also been many calls from politicians to have the Carnival sited in an enclosed park or stadium. This has always been resisted by organisers who believe that it would change the character of Carnival.

In 1986 the police introduced a new strategy with their control room 'Gold Control' co-ordinating 'Silver' and 'Bronze' divisions in the field. More streets were closed to traffic and streets in which reserve forces were kept were open only to residents. The police mingling with the crowd were instructed to turn a blind eye to minor offences. Only when large gangs started to operate did the police intervene. Yet in 1987 the number of crimes reached, as far as the police were concerned, unacceptable levels and confrontations developed after an attempted arrest. By the end of the Carnival there had been 798 reported crimes, 243 arrests (60 for the possession of offensive weapons), and 13 police officers and 76 civilians had been injured, most from gang attacks. There were the usual calls for the Carnival to be stopped and particular criticisms were aimed at organisers for providing too few stewards. In the following year there was further criticism of the organisers in a Coopers and Lybrand report paid for by the Commission for Racial Equality. The debates were concerned with the financial management of the event and the attempts to control events on the ground. Differences between various organisers over the way the Carnival should be run further complicated issues. There were no major problems at the 1988 Carnival and before the event in 1989 a new Carnival Enterprise Committee signed an agreement with the police defining the procession route, the roads to be closed, the positioning of sound systems and the time the Carnival was to close down. The Carnival was very successful until close down on the second day when a confrontation developed. The police later accepted some criticism that they had been too rigid in clearing the streets and had failed to communicate their plans to the crowd. They also agreed to replace the invasive police helicopters with a surveillance airship.

The re-organisation of the running and policing of Carnival had a fundamental influence on the event itself. The number of sound systems was cut dramatically, Carnival was restricted to daylight hours and the parade route was differentiated from the areas where stationary sound systems were placed. The police established 'sterile areas' or 'safety zones' which allow them to move around freely and also meant that police reserves, necessary to control public order, could remain largely out of view. Many saw the controls as too strict and the numbers fell in 1990. There were also fears that the commercialisation of Carnival might transform the event into something akin to the Lord Mayor's Show, and there was heated debate over the 'ownership' and origins of the event. 'Traditionalists' argued that commercialisation was changing the nature of the event and was removing it from the people of the area (Cohen 1993:74-78; Waddington 1994).

During the 1990s Carnival has further developed with sponsors providing greater funding. Since 1995 Carnival has been sponsored by the makers of the soft drink Lilt, owned by Coca Cola. There has been a greater involvement by large companies and radio stations, including BBC Radio 1 and Kiss FM, in the running of sound systems and staging live performances. By 1997 Carnival had become more ethnically diverse: Latin American, Asian and European influences have combined with West Indian and African to make the event a major tourist attraction. Compared to the 1980s there has been a reduction in crimes and there are almost no serious public order incidents. Programmes are available showing the parade routes and listing all the events taking place and maps attached to lampposts also provide information for the bemused spectator. Problems with spectator flow and crushing which were severe on a number of occasions in the 1980s have also greatly reduced.

Carnival has developed within particular social, economic and political relations in London. It may have drawn upon Trinidadian styles, but a combination of factors has meant that it has developed, and will continue to develop, its own distinctive form. Carnival has become a larger and more successful event, yet for some the changes have not been for the better believing the commercialism and organisation have taken the Carnival away from the participants and reduced its spontaneity. And yet it could also be argued that such changes have ensured the survival of the event. Carnival developed in an area of poor housing but Notting Hill has now become more desirable with new residents voicing concerns about their property. The organisers have had the difficult task of addressing the fears of local residents. Had police and organisers not developed a good working relationship one wonders how long Carnival would have lasted in that part of west London.

Celebration and Control

Carnival is difficult to organise and control. Cohen describes it as a 'a celebration of disorder', that its essence is 'chaotic' (1993:69). It can not be expected that organisers should be responsible for all that takes place. The police have a duty to ensure public safety but too much control, too much policing, and too many restrictions are counter-productive and impinge upon the nature of Carnival. In many ways there is no harder event for the authorities to deal with since much in Carnival is about taking away the normal structures of society, removing inhibitions, and empowering individuals in the area in which they live. The rules of the street that normally govern the busy roads of Notting Hill are over-turned.

Over the past thirty years there have been many who would have liked to see Carnival either stopped altogether or restricted to a stadium or enclosed park. The organisers have had to fight for the right for Carnival to take place. At the same time the police and the local authority have had ongoing concerns about Carnival ranging from issues of public order to concerns over public health. In addition, as the nature of the area has changed the interests of some local residents have also changed, and whilst Carnival organisers have not always been able to satisfy some concerns, they have been well aware that it is partly their responsibility to look at issues that might arise. As such the Carnival takes place in a political environment in which there exist a whole range of different interests. There are five areas that appear to be particularly relevant in comparing Carnival with parades in Northern Ireland: liaison, police/organiser co-ordination, stewarding, residents and resources.

Liaison: Relationships between the local authority, the police, other public agencies, residents and organisers has never been easy and even in 1997 there were disagreements and problems. Since the late 1980s those organisations involved in the event have signed a 'Statement of Intent and Code of Practice' which, though not legally binding, acts to create a common understanding over the conduct of the various agencies involved. The code of practice specifies such things as agreed routes, noise levels, close down times, safety zones and pedestrian only zones, the licensing of street traders, and the placing of road signs, while the 1996 Statement of Intent suggested that signatories would:

- Manage the processional route so as to ensure the maximum public safety for people attending the event.
- Ensure a trouble-free Carnival to assure its continuance, by deterring criminal activity and maintaining the Queen's Peace.
- Facilitate the safe passage to and from the event of carnivalists and other people attending.
- Provide a co-ordinated stance to Carnival by Local Authorities, Notting Hill Carnival Ltd., the police, and other parties involved in the event.
- Aim to prevent any unnecessary noise, disturbance or obstruction to residents during the Carnival period.

There are also regular meetings between different agencies, although a liaison group including residents and the Chamber of Commerce broke down in the last year. Public meetings to allow organisers to liaise with residents are held annually. That is not to say that relations have run smoothly but it has certainly given interest groups the ability to make their difficulties known.

<u>Police/Organiser Co-ordination:</u> A central feature of the changes that have taken place at Carnival has been the relations between the police and organisers. In the 1970s and 1980s Carnival acted as a barometer for racial tensions in the city. There is no doubt that over the last ten years the Metropolitan Police have placed considerable efforts on trying to improve the situation. A special section was set up which deals with Carnival all year round and those officers work closely with the organisers, sharing information and resources.

The structure of management on the day involving police and organisers has also developed over the years. The police have a command structure that liaises with the organisers at the different levels. The 'Gold' control centre used to be at a local school which particularly suited organisers but it is now located at Scotland Yard. The police have an officer at the Carnival office and there is a phone line which residents can call if they have any problems. Carnival itself is divided into particular sectors in which officers co-ordinate with organisers in their particular area. By maximising communication at all levels it becomes possible to minimise the chance of misunderstanding the actions of either participants or police officers.

<u>Stewarding:</u> In an ideal situation much of the control of Carnival would be done by stewards. Good stewarding means that the police can be less visible without reducing public safety. At present between 120 and 170 stewards are paid about £90 each and given food and a uniform. The stewards are trained by the police and other emergency services prior to the event. Forty-five stewards, known as Route Managers, are responsible for the movement of the Carnival procession. Each steward is allocated a sector, which coincides with the police sectors and the chief steward liaises with the officer in charge of that sector. It is pointed out to stewards that they must assist police officers and behave responsibly.

Both the organisers and police officers expressed concerns about the reliability of stewards. For stewarding to work well it must strike the correct balance of providing knowledgeable direction without becoming either too authoritarian or getting too involved in the event. There is also an issue as to whether you employ outsiders or locals. It would in principle be possible to hire from agencies that run stewarding at large sports events and rock concerts, but as well as increasing the likelihood of getting insensitive stewarding, it is also expensive. On the other hand, detached outsiders are less likely to get drawn into the revelry of the Carnival. The quality and training of stewards is an ongoing problem, for example one participant felt the stewards did not do enough to protect the floats or the performers. However, the need for good stewarding is recognised by all concerned as an essential requirement for a successful Carnival.

<u>Residents:</u> Many residents look forward to the Carnival and get involved in some way. However, there are contradictions between the right of people to hold a Carnival and the rights of residents to live peacefully, to retain access to the area and to have their property protected. Anyone who has visited Carnival will know how difficult it is to move in and out of the Notting Hill area, how noisy the event can be, and how it can spill from the

streets onto private property. Whilst the organisers recognise some responsibilities and declare sympathy for residents, it would be financially impossible for them to be liable for damage that might be caused. Policy therefore has been aimed at communication and prevention. Public meetings are held at which residents are able to air grievances and at Carnival time a telephone line is available through which residents can contact organisers and police.

Resources: As with all events of this nature money is an issue. How much should an event that can bring in money through sponsorship cost institutions of the state and agencies of the local authority? It costs the local council £100,000 for toilets and £60,000 to clear up afterwards. Notting Hill Carnival Ltd receives some money from Kensington and Chelsea, other London Boroughs, the Arts Council, from sponsorship and franchising and from street trading. But the demands on that money come from both the requirements of agencies to help pay for organising the events and from participants who feel that money should go towards helping them prepare elaborate costumes and floats.

The use of resources is a significant political issue. Organisers, participants, sponsors, local businesses, police and emergency services, local authorities and residents all have different and often competing interests. The objective has been to give people their rights and the facilities to hold the Carnival whilst ensuring public safety and security.

Conclusions

Notting Hill Carnival is a large, complex event that has adapted to changing social circumstances since its inception in the mid-1960s. The event raises a series of issues over rights and responsibilities that are pertinent to issues in Northern Ireland.

Organisers and participants view it as their right to hold the Carnival and it plays an important role in the artistic expression for many within the West Indian community. Yet the event presents difficulties for residents and businesses in the area and creates costs for local and government agencies.

Carnival has become a focus for police community relations over the years. For the Metropolitan Police it is an expensive and difficult event to police, combining as it does a large number of people in confined streets for a somewhat chaotic and anti-authoritarian festival. Carnival has been a focus for the expression of opposition and defiance towards the police, sometimes resulting in significant civil disturbances.

Both the police and organisers have recognised that the future of Carnival depended upon improving the relationship between organisers, participants and police. Since the early 1990s the relations between the police and Notting Hill Carnival Ltd. have been good. This process has not been easy, is not without its critics, and may change in the future, but through good communication and liaison difficult issues over the management of the event have been worked out. Both organisers and the police have had to change the way the Carnival is run and controlled.

A number of methods have developed that have attempted to improve the relationships that surround the Carnival. (i) A Statement of Intent and Code of Practice has been drawn up, which though not legally binding gives those involved an idea of their responsibilities. (ii) Public meetings are held to allow residents to voice their opinions to organisers. (iii) A liaison group worked to try and bring together interested groups. (iv) The police and Carnival organisers work closely together and are prepared to share information.

Changes in the way the Carnival has been organised have allowed the event to attract greater outside funding and sponsorship. Increased commercialisation has changed the event in ways that some have welcomed and others have criticised. The Carnival has attracted an increasingly broad range of people from Britain and abroad.

Management of the Carnival on the day has involved a close, structured, relationship between the police and organisers, the provision of trained stewards, and a telephone line dedicated to problems that residents might have.

The Loyal Orders in Liverpool

Although the Orange Order has never been as strong in England as in Northern Ireland and Scotland, it has played a significant role in the political culture of Liverpool. Like Orange parades in Northern Ireland parades in Liverpool have reflected changing social and political circumstances. In the 1930s concertina bands were prominent in the demonstrations, reflecting the strong maritime links in the city. Until the late 1960s sectarian divisions in the city were such that a Protestant Party was represented on the local council and up to 30,000 people would watch the Twelfth parades with more than one hundred lodges taking part. Members of the loyal orders recount clashes with Catholics in the London Road and Bullring area as recently as 1986. However, the inner city has changed dramatically as a result of slum clearance programmes and many communities have been dispersed to towns outside Liverpool. There are now less than seventy lodges, including women's lodges, in the district.

The Orange Order in the Liverpool and Southport area holds about eighteen parades a year, whilst the Black Institution has four and the Apprentice Boys hold three. All but four of the Orange and Black parades are Sunday church parades, as are two of the three Apprentice Boys parades. By far the largest event is the Twelfth of July in Southport. Three feeder parades take place in Liverpool before Orangemen go to Southport where they meet with other brethren from the north-west for a joint demonstration. There are return parades in Liverpool in the evening. It is customary for two children to be dressed as William and Mary for the day. Members of the Order see the Twelfth in Southport as a family day out.

There are twelve bands in the Liverpool North End area, most are flute bands and are directly connected to Orange lodges in the city. Unlike in Scotland or Northern Ireland members of bands taking part in an Orange parade must be members of the Orange Order but as in Scotland and Northern Ireland bands must follow certain conditions of engagement. These include requirements on types of uniform and the use of regulation marching steps. There are also clauses which requires bands not to play tunes 100 yards either side of a hospital, church or Cenotaph, banning the drinking of alcohol whilst in regalia, and a clause forbidding the playing of party tunes, including the Sash, on a Sunday.

There is also an Independent Orange Order, founded in 1986 after a dispute within the Orange Order over the right to carry 1912 UVF flags. The Independents have less than a dozen parades each year. There are also six independent loyalist bands. These march with both the Apprentice Boys and the Independent Orange Order.

Policing the Parades

Public order legislation requires that seven days notice be given before any procession takes place. However, in Liverpool members of the Orange Order meet with the police as early as February or March to discuss any problems that arose at the previous year's parade and any changes that might be needed. The Order also provides the police with a full list of parades planned for the forthcoming year and a list of the lodges and bands expected at each event.

In general the police felt that problems over parades were being reduced, but they identified a number of issues that remained problematic. The Twelfth parade in Southport is not always easy because there are a lot of holiday makers in the town who know little about Orange parades and who sometimes cause problems if they walk through the ranks of the parade. The police felt that it was not always easy to find a balance between the rights of marchers and the rights of people to go about their business. As such, the police are keen that the Orangemen are aware of this and are patient with the general public. There are also a few problems on the return parades in Liverpool as a number of the people who gather to watch are often the worse for drink. While there is no need to close any roads in Liverpool for the morning processions, they do close two roads in the evening. Although the police like at least one steward for every 50 people, they would be nervous of having stewards deal with anyone not in the procession.

There have been no disputes with local residents since 1986 but the relationship between the Orange Order and Independent Orange Order is so poor that arrangements have to be made to keep the two events separate in both Liverpool and Southport. This means liaising to check that buses do not arrive in Southport at the same time. Also in recent years, there have been problems with fascist groups such as the National Front and Combat 18 attaching themselves to loyal order parades. There were incidents at a pub in Southport in 1996 requiring the use of the riot squad. However, senior members of the Orange Order made it clear that they would not tolerate members of Combat 18 in the Institution and the police believe that C18 just attaches itself to the event to raise its own profile.

In general the changing social circumstances have meant that there are fewer problems over Orange parades in Liverpool than there used to be and relations between the Orders and the police are now very good. In Liverpool many of the customary routes in the city are less populated than they would have been in the past and in Southport the main concerns are with the interests of tourists and local businesses.

Conclusions

As social and political circumstances change the environment in which events are policed can become quite different. In Northern Ireland the policing of Orange parades has become increasingly more problematic with political and residential changes. In Liverpool the events seem to be less tense than in the past and any problems are more to do with crowd control, the use of alcohol and the interests of tourists and businesses. The police were particularly appreciative of the co-operative attitude of the Orange Order in contacting them at the start of the year to make arrangements for forthcoming events.

Scotland

The legal situation in Scotland differs from that in England and Wales. Under the Civic Government (Scotland) Act 1982, notification of a procession should be made to a local council official seven days in advance of the event. There is a provision for processions 'commonly or customarily held' not to have to give formal notification but councils are empowered to waive this provision if they so wish. The council is required to notify the police of any planned parades. The council may prohibit the holding of a procession or impose conditions concerning the date, time and duration of the procession, the route to be taken or to prohibit it from particular public areas. For instance, organisers informed us that in Glasgow the police are keen that there should be no parades after 1.00pm and therefore most parades start before 11.00am and, unlike in Northern Ireland, the police in Glasgow were not keen on the carrying of symbolic weapons such as swords. The council is required to give notice of any restrictions to the organisers two days prior to the event and to publicise them in such a way that participants will be made aware of the conditions.

An appeal can be made to the Sheriff who can uphold the appeal if in his/her opinion the council 'erred in law', had incorrect factual information, were unreasonable in exercising their discretion or acted beyond their powers. The Sheriff may return the case to the council for reconsideration, make an order him/herself or dismiss the appeal. An appeal against the Sheriff's decision, on a point of law, can be made to the Court of Session. A variety of offences exist to deal with individuals who disregard any order made by the authorities.

Perhaps the most significant difference with the situation in England and Wales is the involvement of the local council. The organiser of an event must complete a form in triplicate, one copy goes to the local authority, one to the police and the third, with a code of conduct on the reverse side, is retained by the organiser. The council officer informs the relevant members of the council that a parade is to be held in their area and they have the opportunity to raise any objections. In Glasgow the council has a Public Processions sub-committee to address any problems. The police can make their views known to the council officer and comment on objections, but it is the local authority that makes the formal decision over any restrictions on parades. However on the day the police can invoke public order concerns to change previous decisions.

All of those that we spoke to about the organisation of loyal order parades said that they gave plenty of notice, weeks if not months, before holding a parade. In the main they were perfectly happy with the relationship they had with the police and if necessary would discuss issues in advance.

Orange Parades

Orangeism was brought to Scotland at the end of the eighteenth century by military regiments returning from Ireland and lodges slowly spread through working class areas of Scotland. Just as in Ireland, outbreaks of disorder connected to processions were common. The first Twelfth parade in Glasgow in 1821 ended in disturbances, as they did the following year. In 1823 the magistrates banned the march (Marshall 1996:12-14). The Orange Order expanded with the growth of industrialisation in the second half of the nineteenth century and, whilst the mass of Scottish Orangeism remained working class, it gained in respectability. In particular Orangeism became a distinctive part of political culture in Glasgow.

Changing political and economic circumstances have affected the Orange Order in Scotland and it now holds less political power than it did in the past. Nevertheless, there are still a large number of parades and the Twelfth remains a significant day in certain areas of Scotland. In the Strathclyde area alone the Orange Order held 504 processions and the Black Institution held 54 between 1 July 1995 and 30 June 1996. As in Northern Ireland many of these processions are church parades and most are held between June and August. Four Twelfth processions are held each year on one of the Saturdays preceding the Twelfth: Ayrshire, Glasgow, Central Scotland and East Scotland. The Orange Order estimates that up to 20,000 people attend the Glasgow Twelfth.

Some of the issues that have arisen over Orange parades in Northern Ireland have also created controversy in Scotland. The Twelfth parades have had a reputation for drunkenness and sectarianism. This has meant that attempt by the loyal orders to hold processions in new areas has been met with some opposition from local authorities, as was the case in Aberdeen in 1997. Whilst the right of Orangemen to hold processions in Glasgow is still governed by tradition, the route is not as highly valued as on processions in Northern Ireland. Consequently there have been few problems with residents objecting to the processions. Nevertheless, at least one commentator has suggested that if local authorities continue to restrict processions by republican bands (see below) then the call for greater restrictions on loyal order events, in the name of even-handedness, might grow (Marshall 1996:164). However, problems over the drinking of alcohol and the control of paramilitary displays by bands have been more prominent than the issue of controversial routes.

Alcohol and 'hangers-on'

The consumption of alcohol is possibly more prevalent and has been more of a problem in Scotland than in Northern Ireland. Marshall suggests that 'the Order's public image continues to be marred by the loutish and anti-social behaviour' of supporters lining the streets and accompanying processions. He points out that the Scottish Order in many ways abandoned pretensions towards temperance when they sanctioned the licensing of Orange premises in the 1960s and an increasing number of District premises started to sell alcohol. The allegiance of the clientele of particular pubs either to Orangeism, Unionism and Glasgow Rangers or Irish Republicanism and Glasgow Celtic has long been a distinctive part of Glasgow's social scene. Whilst members of the Order are concerned about images of drunkenness, they feel that in the main it is up to the police to deal with drunken behaviour from anybody that is not actually in the parade itself.

Paramilitary displays

Over recent years the issue that has received most attention inside and outside Scottish Orangeism has been the relationship of the Institution and bands to loyalist paramilitary groups (Bruce 1985; Marshall 1996). In the early 1970s significant numbers of Scottish Orangemen became at least nominal members of the UDA, which at that point was not an illegal organisation. This eventually led to a very divisive split in the Grand Lodge in 1976 resulting in an unequivocal condemnation of 'terrorist organisations'. Concern over the image of Orangeism in Scotland has remained an issue within the Orange Order and the dispute surfaced again over displays of paramilitarism by loyalist bands taking part in Orange processions. During a Twelfth parade in Buxburn in 1989 the Young Cowdenbeath Volunteers Flute Band appeared in replica uniforms of the Young Citizens Volunteers, the youth section of the UVF. The band were banned from participating in any further Orange parades and in the resulting dispute a lodge had its warrant suspended. In similar disputes in the following years, other lodges were suspended for hiring paramilitary style bands. Those lodges have now formed the Independent Orange Order in Scotland.

One of the reasons for the hard line taken by the Orange Order is due to concern over the possibility of restrictions on parades by the police who, in Glasgow at least, make their officers well aware of the flags of proscribed organisations. The Order has dealt with the problem in two ways. First, all bands taking part in parades under Grand Lodge jurisdiction must be members of either the Scottish Amateur Flute Band Association, the Scottish Accordion Band Association or one of the four sections of the First Flute Band Association which is effectively run by the Orange Order. Bands from outside jurisdictions, such as Northern Ireland, can only take part by producing a letter of recommendation from a private or district Orange lodge in their area. In recent years at least one band from Belfast has been banned because of its conduct on a parade in Scotland.

In effect the Orange Order in Scotland run a band registration system to control the behaviour of bands and also the symbolic content of Orange parades. It has been suggested that a similar system should be set up in Northern Ireland and there has long been provision within legislation for the registration of bands. Experience in Scotland suggests that if organisers of events are to take responsibility for their parades, then they should act to register participants.

The second way the Scottish Orange Order have sought to improve the control of their events is by using a detailed band contract. The contract designates the type of uniforms bands should wear; that there should be only one bass drummer; the size of bass drum; the types of flags to be displayed - with a maximum of three flags (of which one must be the Union flag and the second either the Scottish Soltire or the flag of the bands jurisdiction); that there should be no paramilitary insignia; a band cannot have a name with the initials YCV; the tune The Wild Colonial Boy should never be played; that there should be no unseemly shouting; that only regulation marching step should be used; that there should be no drinking or playing of music by bands at the Field, that bands should not carry deacon poles or batons; and that bands on church parades must attend the service and only play hymns. The Orange Order in Northern Ireland has a similar contract, although it is not quite as specific as that used by the brethren in Scotland.

The Grand Lodge also controls the fees that the bands get for being engaged by the lodges, which some might see as a bit of localised restrictive practice. Such a degree of control has not been popular with all the bands nor with all members of the Order. Nevertheless, the overall effect of the use of band associations and band contracts has been to allow the Grand Lodge the ability to control better what takes place in Orange parades.

Apprentice Boys

The Apprentice Boys Clubs were first established in Scotland in 1903, but the development of the association in Scotland was slow compared to that of Orangeism. The first Apprentice Boys parade appears not to have taken place until 1959 and an annual parade has since taken place on the third Saturday of May. The number of clubs has increased since the start of the troubles in Northern Ireland and they are now formed under Scottish Amalgamated Committee. Most, but not all, members of the Apprentice Boys will be in the Orange Order, however, the two institutions have no official links and the Apprentice Boys have a reputation for supporting more militant loyalism, whereas the Orange Order does not. Between 1 July 1995 and 30 June 1996 there were 55 Apprentice Boys Parades in the Strathclyde area.

One of the principal differences between the Apprentice Boys and the Orange Order in Scotland has been over the treatment of bands. The Apprentice Boys do not dictate to bands what flags they may or may not carry, and they are prepared to let bands that have been banned by the Orange Order into their parades. For instance, the Apprentice Boys allow flags connected to the 36th Ulster Division to be flown whereas the Orange Order acknowledges the importance of the Ulster Division, but does not see it as relevant to Scottish Orangeism. Apprentice Boys that we spoke to take the position that if the police did not have a problem with particular flags, then it was not for the loyal orders to dictate what was carried.

The police usually did not stop the traffic for their parades so it was important they kept to the correct side of the road. The Apprentice Boys appointed marshals to stop people going through the ranks and to keep the parade on the correct part of the road. Any problems with 'hanger's on' they felt were for the police to deal with.

Republican Parades

There have long been events reflecting Irish nationalism in Scotland, often displayed through processions organised by the Ancient Order of Hibernians. However, since the 1970s a number of specifically republican events have been held regularly. We were told that there are around twelve republican bands in the Glasgow area within the Irish Scottish Bands Association (ISBA). Most events take place within areas which are broadly Roman Catholic and, unlike the Orange Order, they would not, generally, be allowed into Glasgow city centre. Nevertheless, some of the republican parades have been attracting the attention of militant loyalists who are prepared to try to stop such events.

Police in Strathclyde said that they had had relatively few problems. On one occasion when loyalist and republican parades wanted to organise in the same area, it was sorted out by changing the starting times; the longer-established loyalist parade was not given precedent. However, there have been more serious problems in other areas. In 1995 the ISBA were refused a parade in Blantyre on the basis that there had been trouble in previous years. ISBA then applied filed for a parade each week for some months, invoking their right to march, and causing some administrative problems. They were asked to stop applying on the basis that after a bit of time they would be given a parade, which eventually took place. In 1996 republican bands in Paisley, Renfrewshire made an application to march under the heading 'Ban the RUC'. Neither the local council nor the police objected, but after the local paper suggested that there might be sectarian clashes, the council withdrew approval. The ISBA did not appeal to the Sheriff. In Edinburgh, where an annual march for republican socialist James Connolly takes place, there have probably been more problems with both republican and loyalist events than in Glasgow (Marshall1996:164). A number of local authorities have refused permission to republican groups partly because of the threat of counter demonstrations from militant loyalists. Marshall believes that there has been a deliberate attempt by a group of loyalists to target republican parades, however he points out that this could have the effect of reducing tolerance towards Orange parades in Scotland.

Conclusions

Scotland, and specifically Glasgow, provided some of the most obvious comparisons with Northern Ireland over the type of parades that take place. Yet the legal provisions for controlling parades offer interesting contrasts with those in England and Northern Ireland. In England the police are principal decision-makers over parades, whereas in Scotland a council official co-ordinates the decision making process on behalf of the local authority and there is a clear line of appeal if a decision is disputed.

The differing relationships with the state have also influenced attitudes to the right to parade. In Northern Ireland the relationship of the Orange Order with the Unionist Party and the RUC enabled Orange parades to establish and maintain 'traditional' routes. The present disputes over such routes are seen as a threat to sovereignty and power. In Scotland the Order had some political power, but not on the same scale as in Northern Ireland, and furthermore there is no threat of any sort of Catholic state. Orangeism has therefore been less forceful in demanding 'traditional' rights. Alteration to a route is not so easily perceived as a reduction in the civil rights of Orangemen, who have never dominated the public sphere in the way that their brethren have in Northern Ireland.

Holding parades is a part of Scottish political culture and the authorities accept that some parades, such as the Twelfth, should have precedent because they are long established or 'traditional'. Nevertheless, both organisers and the authorities accept that specific roads are not sacrosanct and the right to hold a parade on a particular day does not mean the right to march over the same route every year. The right to hold a traditional parade is important, not the right to use a traditional route.

Issues of the right to parade have not loomed large in Scottish politics. The loyal orders have accepted those occasions when local authorities have refused permission for parades to take place and the small number of republican events have in the main not demanded routes that were likely to create an issue. However, there have been attempts by loyalists to stop republican events and concern has been expressed that this might reduce public toleration of Orange parades.

The loyal orders have had problems with public perceptions of their events, particularly given the prevalence of the consumption of alcohol on occasions such as the Twelfth. A cursory review suggests that the situation may be worse than it is in Northern Ireland due in part to the more relaxed attitude of the Scottish Orangeism to the licensing of their premises.

Disputes over paramilitary symbols and insignia have been more prevalent in Scotland than in Northern Ireland. The police have taken a harder line than their counterparts in Northern Ireland and senior Orangemen have argued against the carrying of paramilitary insignia in Orange parades. The Orange Order in Scotland has played a more pro-active role in controlling the symbols within its parades.

An important difference between Scotland and Northern Ireland has been the control of bands. In Scotland the registration of bands has been organised by the Orange Order, allowing them to expel any band not conforming to codes of behaviour and dress. Loyalist bands in Northern Ireland probably play a more dominant role in street political culture than do their counterparts in Scotland and senior Orangemen in Northern Ireland have felt unable to take some of the steps to control the bands that they claim should be made and have tended to argue that it is the responsibility of the state to deal with this issue rather than the organisers of the relevent event.

Republic of Ireland

Disputes over parades and demonstrations have not been a persistent factor in recent Irish social life. However, they have been cause of serious public disorder on a small number of occasions. Following partition in 1921 there were a number of disputes over Orange parades in the border counties and in the 1930s Eamon de Valera was sufficiently concerned about the growth of IRA activity to declare the organisation unlawful and their commemorations and assemblies were banned or constrained (Jarman & Bryan 1998). In 1939 the Offences Against the State Act which allows widespread restrictions on public assemblies was passed.

More recently the two occasions at which serious disorder has broken out in Dublin resulted from political protests. In February 1972 the British Embassy in Dublin was burnt down following a demonstration protesting at the Bloody Sunday killings. In July 1981 extensive rioting followed another march on the Embassy, this time in protest at the British Government's stance on the IRA Hunger Strikes. There was criticism of the decision to allow the march to take place in the first place, but the Government defended the right to peaceful protest. Furthermore, it indicated that in spite of the violence it saw no reason to ban a similar march planned for the following week (Brewer et al 1996:100). The Minister for Justice, Mr Mitchell, stated that 'the government's predisposition will be not to interfere with the right to peaceful protest' and he said that marches should only be banned 'as a very last resort'. Extra police were on duty the following Saturday but the march passed off peacefully (**Irish Times** 20.7.1981, 27.7.1981).

The most recent dispute arose in August 1986 in the wake of parading disputes in Portadown and over the Anglo-Irish Agreement. Peter Robinson of the Democratic Unionist Party led an estimated one hundred and fifty loyalists on a night-time sortie to the County Monaghan village of Clontibret. Having occupied the village the men painted slogans on the local Garda barracks, damaged cars and attacked two Gardai before being dispersed by plain-clothes officers who fired over the heads of the crowd. Robinson was arrested and charged under the Offences Against the State Act. He later pleaded guilty to unlawful assembly (**Irish News** 8.8.1986, 9.8.1986, 17.1.1987).

Two conclusions can be made from these few brief details. First that there has been little controversy or conflict over the right to hold parades as such, and after the most recent and most serious of the disturbances the government was keen to reiterate and confirm the importance of the right to demonstrate. Second, each of the examples of disputes have been related to the conflict in the North rather than being related to issues internal to the state (although the dispute with the IRA in the 1930s blurs this distinction somewhat).

Constitutional Rights

The right to freedom of assembly was incorporated in the initial Constitution of the Irish state (Article 9) and today is guaranteed by Article 40.6.1.ii and 2 of the revised Irish Constitution of 1937 (Kelly 1980). This states that

The State guarantees liberty for the exercise, subject to public order and morality, of the right of the citizens to assemble peacefully and without arms.

Provision may be made by law to prevent or control meetings which are determined in accordance with law to be calculated to cause a breach of the peace or to be a danger or nuisance to the general public and to prevent or control meetings in the vicinity of either House of the Oireachtas.

Laws regulating the manner in which ... the right of free assembly may be exercised shall contain no political, religious or class discrimination.

While this indicates that freedom of assembly is recognised as an important civil right, the Constitution also clearly indicates that such a right is not unlimited. It can be qualified and subject to restrictions over concerns for both public order and morality. However, because the issue of parades and demonstrations has not been a contentious matter since the 1930s, there is little in the way of legal authority on the meaning or interpretation of the Constitutional right to assembly: 'Apart from trade union cases, all the principal reported Irish authorities on public meetings and demonstrations pre-date the Constitution' (Forde 1987:484). Most of these authorities in fact date from before partition and are based on British legal jurisdiction (Kelly 1980).

Legal Constraints

The Constitution explicitly permits some legal restraints to be placed on the right to assembly and specifically when there is a threat to public order. A number of subsequent Acts have empowered the Garda Siochana to ban assemblies in certain circumstances.

- The Offences Against the State Act, 1939, provides for a blanket prohibition on meetings or processions 'by or on behalf of or by arrangement or in concert with an unlawful organisation' (S.27).
- The same act also permits a senior Garda officer to prohibit any meetings or procession within half a mile of a building in which either House of the Oireachtas is sitting or is about to sit (S.28).
- The Road Traffic Act, 1961, prohibits any act which might cause the obstruction of traffic, and could therefore be used to restrain demonstrations (Forde 1987).
- The Offences Against the State (Amendment) Act, 1972, makes any meeting or procession which interferes with, directly or indirectly, the course of justice an unlawful assembly.
- The Criminal Justice (Public Order) Act, 1994, replaced a number of common law offences relating to public order and also gave Gardai extended powers of crowd control. Wilful obstruction involves preventing or interrupting the free passage of person or vehicle in a public place (S.9), while the common law offences of riot, rout and unlawful assembly were replaced by statutory offences of riot or violent disorder (Ss.14 & 15).

Violent disorder involves 'three or more people' who 'use or threaten to use unlawful violence' which makes 'a person of reasonable firmness' fear for his or another person's safety. Under existing practice the Gardai can disperse such an assembly but only by using force which is 'moderate and proportioned to the circumstances' (Forde 1987, Doolan 1994).

- The Act also gives a Garda 'not below the rank of superintendent' power to control access to public events 'in the interests of safety or for the purpose of preserving order' (S.21) and to control the consumption of alcohol in such areas (S.22). While this part of the legislation seems to have been aimed at sporting events, pop concerts and the like it could also be applied to political rallies and demonstrations.

Although legislation allows for some degree of constraint on the freedom of assembly the law has rarely been called into use at parades or demonstrations. Senior members of the Garda Siochana who deal with public assemblies in Dublin stated that while it was possible to invoke the Road Traffic and Public Order Acts to constrain parades, to their knowledge they had not been invoked. Similarly, although they were able to prohibit demonstrations in the vicinity of the Dail, nobody had been prevented from holding such a demonstration since 1966 when a man was arrested and prosecuted for participating in an illegal protest by farmers. It was subsequently decided that it would be better to permit peaceful demonstrations rather than risk the area becoming a regular site of contentious illegal protests. Large numbers of demonstrations and protests are held in the vicinity of the Dail each year without causing any trouble.

However there is some concern that the Criminal Justice (Public Order) Act, 1994, might be used to control some forms of political demonstration. In May 1997 a Socialist Worker Party candidate was arrested under the breach of the peace provisions while campaigning for the Dail elections. A spokesperson for the Irish Council of Civil Liberties subsequently claimed that the new law had been 'widely used on individuals engaged in political and protest activity' (**Irish Times** 12-6-1997).

Practice

While there is a Constitutional right to freedom of assembly, it must also be balanced with the rights of others to use public space. There is no requirement that organisers notify the police or any other agents of the state of their intentions, but the Garda Siochana are responsible for maintaining public order and freedom of movement more generally. In the early years of the troubles there was little contact between the Gardai and the republican movement over parades and demonstrations, by the 1980s communication had been improved but there remains something of a rivalry over control of traffic at parades. Sinn Féin like their own stewards to take responsibility, while the Gardai are equally keen to retain control of the streets. The Garda Siochana encourage proper stewarding by the organisers, but they are also concerned that their own role in maintaining order should not be usurped.

Most groups do notify the Gardai of their intentions to hold a demonstration and, even if they are not informed the Gardai usually find out in advance: 'all parades and protests need publicity of some kind'. A republican demonstration in Letterkenny, in response to events at Drumcree in July 1996, did take the local Gardai by surprise, but fewer people than expected turned up and they were able to deal with it adequately.

In most cases the Gardai take the initiative and contact the organisers of events to discuss the proposals for the route, and the time, the scale and the nature of the event. Although they have no powers to prohibit parades, or to impose formal conditions, they can influence the route that is taken and the timing of the event. In most cases their main concern is with maintaining the flow of traffic, although on occasion they have had to deal with competing demands for demonstrations over the same route at the same time. Usually an acceptable compromise is reached but Gardai stated that they were aware that if a group insists on their right to demonstrate where and when they want then they have little power to stop them.

Parades in Donegal

County Donegal draws more strongly than other areas on the Northern custom of parading; the county hosts a diverse range of parades and demonstrations each year. St Patrick's Day is widely marked in towns and villages, although usually by small events, a well attended Easter Commemoration is held at Dunglow and smaller commemorations recur elsewhere. There are also a number of parades organised by the loyal orders. Many of these are feeder parades and are held prior to main anniversaries in the North; others are local church parades. The largest annual event in Donegal is the Orange Order parade in Rossnowlagh in early July. The Gardai usually talk to representatives of the local lodge some months in advance of the parade. They want to know the numbers of lodges and bands that are expected so that they can plan the policing requirements, although on the day this amounts to little more than organising traffic control. The Guards have no power to impose formal conditions on the parade, but informal agreements have been established over acceptable practices with regard to flags and bands. At the 1997 parade about 4,000 people took part in the parade, while there were no Union flags, there were six Ulster flags and a similar number of Orange Standards carried.

There have never been any public order problems at the Rossnowlagh parade but echoes of the Northern Irish parade disputes have been felt elsewhere in the county in recent years. In July and August 1996 small protests were mounted at returning parades in Convoy and Manorcunningham, while a march and rally protesting about events at Drumcree was held in Letterkenny (**Derry People and Donegal News** 12.7, 19.7.1996). In Convoy the local Orange lodge re-routed their parade to avoid confrontation while in August the Manorcunningham branch of the Apprentice Boys ignored the protests and walked their normal route. In March 1997 sectarian graffiti was painted in Dunkinnealy prior to a Boys Brigade parade and a similar incident occurred in Ballintra prior to the Rossnowlagh parade in July. In the first case the parade was cancelled, while in Ballintra the graffiti was painted over and the morning church parade went ahead as planned. In neither of the cases was a physical protest mounted. However, a small crowd of demonstrators did try to stop an

Orange parade in St Johnston on the Twelfth, but Gardai ensured that the parade was able to take place (**Derry People and Donegal News** 18.7.1997). To date these protests have been small in scale, largely peaceful and easily controlled by the Garda Siochana. There is nothing to suggest that they will escalate in scale.

Conclusions

The history of parading in Ireland can be dated back at least as far as the fifteenth century and at times of political transformation parades and demonstrations have been the focus of contention and conflict. The extent to which this has not been a factor in recent decades can be discerned in part from the absence of any constitutional reviews to the basic rights to assembly and in part from lack of clear legal powers with which the Garda Siochana can control public gatherings.

The most recent murmurings of disputes are but a small reflection of the contention the subject has generated in the North. To date they have not shown any signs of escalating, an indication of the declining social significance of the loyal orders in the Republic, where their parades really are little more than apolitical and non-contentious customs.

At present the Garda are able to deal with the minor disputes over the 'time, place and manner' in which parades are held through an informal process of dialogue and compromise. While there is recognition of the significance of the Constitutional guarantee of freedom of peaceful assembly, there is also a practical acknowledgement that such rights are not absolute and must also bear in mind the rights of others.

Furthermore while at present the state is able to accommodate the level of demand for the right to public assembly, it has nevertheless introduced legislation that could be used to restrict the practical expression of those rights. To date it has not needed to use those legal powers.

France

Demonstrations are very much a feature of French political life. They would fit comfortably between the beret and the snail on the list of French stereotypes, and many foreigners who have lived in or travelled through the country would have borne away images of political demonstrations, strikes, pickets and road blocks that they have encountered.

There is an average of eight demonstrations a day in Paris according to the *préfecture de police*, the department of the police who are responsible for all public gatherings. These mainly consist of small-scale protests although larger rallies and protests do bring the country to a standstill on a regular basis. Major political issues can mobilise a million or more people on to the streets of the capital and the main cities. The student protests of May 1968 remain the key examples of large-scale protest and those events have had a long-standing impact on both the politics and the social development of contemporary France.

Demonstrations in France differ significantly from the type of parades held in Northern Ireland mainly because they are almost exclusively issue related. State commemorations, such as Bastille Day (14 July) or Armistice Day (11 November), are probably the only real 'traditional' parades, while longstanding anniversaries such as May Day, organised by the trade unions invariably have a contemporary political message. The vast majority of demonstrations would be a form of political protest and it could be argued that in France the right to demonstrate is understood as a right to express an opinion rather than to celebrate a cultural or religious tradition.

Although rising unemployment and a decline in the power and importance of the trade unions have led to a reduction in large demonstrations in recent years they can still play a very important social and political role as has been evident during recent strikes by farmers and lorry drivers. Large assemblies and protests have often persuaded the government to reconsider their position or their policies and they are still an element of most negotiating processes. The size and number of marches constitutes a reliable social indicator. A million people on the street give negotiators a very powerful mandate when dealing with the government. On the other hand calling for a demonstration on a serious issue can only be done provided enough people will be mobilised. A 'failed' demonstration, explained a trade unionist, would give a green light for a government to go ahead with whatever contentious project it wants to force through.

The right to demonstrate is strongly established and well protected in France and poses few problems. Even if France is not the human rights haven it claims to be, people are still proud of this image and hold a belief in the importance of human rights very dear. People would be very protective in terms of their rights and freedoms, and would be likely to protest against the banning of a demonstration that they would not have been part of in the first place. However, taking a closer look at the situation in terms of the legislation and the experiences of diverse groups reveals many practices that muddy the picture. For example, disputes over rallies organised by the neo-fascist *Front National* have been confronted by public opposition and counter demonstrations and have opened an interesting debate in terms of civil liberties.

Legal Framework

The right to demonstrate is not entrenched in the Constitution and is not even positively defined by the law but rather is only implicitly protected by the *Nouveau Code Pénal*. Article 431-1 of the *Code* allows for punishment for concerted obstruction to 'freedom of expression, work, association, meeting or demonstration' (Morange 1997). This therefore also gives legal status to freedom of assembly and the right to demonstrate.

The current legislation relating to the right to demonstrate is based on a *décret loi* introduced in 1935 following violent clashes between fascist and communist groups. The *décret loi 23-10-1935* requires the organisers of a demonstration to notify the authorities of their plans at least three days before the event is due to take place. In Paris the central office of the *prèfecture de police* co-ordinate all activities related to parades, demonstrations and other public assemblies. The *préfet* himself is directly responsible to the *Ministre de l'Interieur*, while four *commissaires* are responsible for the administration of gatherings. In smaller towns this work would be carried out through the office of the mayor.

Notification of any proposed assembly must include the date, time, place, intended route and purpose of the demonstration as well as the name and address of three organisers. Although assemblies do not need 'authorisation', notification is nonetheless compulsory and a parade that has not been notified to the police authority is therefore an illegal event. Parades whose aim is considered to threaten the institutions of the Republic or infringe upon the law are also considered illegal.

Imposing Conditions

Demonstrations can be banned by the *préfet* if it is felt that public order or other fundamental liberties such as freedom of movement, to work or to enjoy private property are at risk. The *préfet* must presume that there is both a real threat to public order and that there is no other available means to avoid that trouble (Pontier 1997). Few parades are in effect banned and many parades do take place without advanced notification. The limited number of interdictions is mainly due to the fact that the *préfet* can impose a range of partial changes or specific restrictions. Amongst other things he/she can ask for a modification of the route, the time, and the date. In France the right to demonstrate does not amount to a right to march anywhere at any given time.

Whilst there have been difficulties in Northern Ireland over the issue of 'traditional' routes, this has never been the case in France as traditional routes simply do not exist. Although there are particular areas of Paris in which parades and demonstrations are regularly held there is no special symbolic status linking certain organisations to any one route nor any specific right to demonstrate in any one place.

Prohibitions are usually challenged before a *juge administratif*. During times of public unrest or when public order has been at risk the police authorities have not hesitated to ban parades. The *juges administratifs* have generally upheld such decisions, although on occasions police decisions to ban a demonstration have been declared illegal (*cf: CE, sect. 19.02.54 Union des synd. ouvriers de la règion parisienne CGT et sieur Hènaff; 21.06.72: Sieurs Malisson* [Long, Weil & Braiban 1984]). However, the impact of these decisions is only one of 'principle' since they were made several years after the contentious parade was due to take place. In practice the decision of the *prèfet* is effectively final.

The *Code Pénal* lists a number of illegal activities that can occur around demonstrations and that can lead to prosecution. It establishes first of all a distinction between legal or authorised demonstrations and unlawful assemblies or *attroupements* (article 431-3 of the *Code Pénal*). An *attroupement* is an assembly that is held without prior notification and which also threatens public order. A spontaneous parade resulting from a peaceful gathering does not therefore necessarily constitute an *attroupement*. Demonstrations and peaceful assemblies can disintegrate into unlawful assemblies at any time and can then be dispersed by force after two warnings have been given. However as is the case in other jurisdictions, the criteria for judging the nature of public order and the seriousness of threats to it are extremely vague. Therefore the legislation basically authorises the police to disperse any spontaneous demonstration if they deem it to be necessary.

Organising a demonstration without prior notification, or organising a demonstration that has been banned, carry penalties of up to six months imprisonment and a 50,000 FF. fine (c£5,000). Anyone participating in either legal or illegal demonstrations carrying a weapon (including spades, projectiles etc.) can be imprisoned for three years, while inciting an armed assembly is liable to seven years imprisonment. Non-nationals moreover face a possible exclusion order for any of the above offences.

The local authorities have customarily been held financially responsible for any damages caused during demonstrations or riots, although public authorities can sue individuals whose responsibility can be proved. Following the extensive rioting in 1968, the government introduced 'anti-riot' legislation (*loi anticasseurs*), which placed responsibility for any damages with the organisers of the demonstration. However this law was repealed in 1981.

Practice

French law distinguishes between demonstrations that are authorised and legal and those that have been banned. In practice however, most parades follow a third scenario where the right to demonstrate exists only with substantial restrictions which are imposed or agreed following negotiations with the *prèfet*. After receiving initial notification of the intention to hold a demonstration, the *prèfet* invites the organisers to discuss the details of the event. If demonstrators want to march along busy streets at a busy time then the police can insist on a change of the timing or of the entire route. The *prèfet* must always take into account the potential disruption to the economic life of different areas and will try to spread the various demonstrations throughout the day, the week, and the main arteries of Paris.

When a compromise is agreed, the *prèfet* and the organisers jointly sign a form that lists both the conditions that have been established and a summary of the current legislation governing parades. Although this document has no legal basis, it is described as a contract between the two parties: the organisers promise to follow the agreed terms while the police now have a responsibility to provide security along the route of the parade.

The quality of the contact between organisers and the *prèfecture* varies considerably and depends on how 'professional' the group organising the demonstration is. Major trade unions and radical groups like Act Up, who have established themselves as perpetual demonstrators, have regular contacts with civil servants in the *préfecture* and talk of a good working relationship. The *préfecture* explained how organisers have sometimes informed them of what was likely to happen during a demonstration: how far the demonstrators would expect to go and to what extent they would accept restrictions without feeling compromised. An unspoken agreement can come out of such meetings ensuring the credibility of the organisers and effective control by the police over the events. The majority of demonstrators are unaware of the negotiations which have taken place behind closed doors and what will often look like an infringement on the agreed contract might very well be the result of an informal agreement. Smaller, less 'demonstration orientated' groups who would not attract the same number of people in the street do not have the same ability to get their way since removing a small number of demonstrators from a busy street can be easier for the police than disrupting the traffic.

The police responsibility for the security of a legal parade is demonstrated by the presence of a police vehicle at the head of the procession. If that demonstration is likely to meet little opposition, the police presence will be minimal and restricted to traffic control along the route. The police make a point of minimising their presence as much as possible and expect the organisers to take substantial responsibility for a peaceful event. The organisers of a demonstration usually walk in front of the ordinary marchers and are therefore positioned between the demonstrators and the police. This allows for easy communication in the event of trouble or problems arising and also allows the organisers to distance themselves from being held responsible in case rioting breaks out. Once the demonstration is over, the organisers must call for its dispersion, the police are then responsible for the situation.

Demonstrations organised by well-established groups generally provide their own stewards. Even though it is not a legal requirement, the police expect some internal security to be arranged by the group itself and there is often a tacit agreement between the two parties in terms of delegating security powers to the stewards. Such a delegation of authority is formally prohibited and could certainly be legally challenged, although it would most likely be argued that the stewards have only natural authority over other demonstrators. However recently problems have occurred with the *Front National* whose stewards are dressed in police-style uniforms, often try to check people's identification and have violently confronted counter-demonstrators. These issues have arisen in part because the FN have argued that as the police have not been willing to protect their rights they will have to do it themselves. At present it is not a serious problem, but it does raise issues about the appropriate limits to informal stewarding of demonstrations.

Policing Demonstrations

The policing of demonstrations has been a recurring issue throughout French history. The army was traditionally in charge of restoring order, but as a result of problems relating to both fraternisation and inadequate training. Conscription meant that local soldiers frequently knew the demonstrators, conversely at other times the reaction of the army was often too violent and they opened fire on unarmed civilians on several occasions. It was therefore decided to create a 'normal' police force that would be specially trained to deal with crowd control. This led to the creation of the *Compagnies Républicaines de Sécurité* (CRS) in 1945. It was thought that such a force would be more likely to try to avoid bloodshed and would more adequately balance the needs of maintaining public order and avoiding risk to life.

The way in which a demonstration is policed depends largely on the threat it is perceived to present to public order. Most parades or assemblies only require the assistance of ordinary police personnel whose role will be limited to control of the traffic. The CRS are attached to the police department under the authority of the Home Secretary. They will generally be mobilised in the vicinity of demonstrations but out of sight of the demonstrators. The CRS will be called upon if a demonstration is likely to meet some opposition, tries to take a forbidden route, or if public order needs to be restored. Their officers receive special public order and crowd control training. If the police experience extra difficulty, it is possible to call on the *gendarmes mobiles*, although this would mainly occur in times of generalised strikes and widespread demonstrations. Even though they are military personnel, the *gendarmes mobiles* have a similar training to the CRS and wear comparable uniforms. When working with the police, military personnel are always expected to follow police orders.

The *Renseignements Généraux* (RG) who are responsible for police intelligence play a major role in the organising of the policing of demonstrations. They give the police authority information on the conditions surrounding the planned demonstration, thus allowing the prèfet to evaluate the necessary police presence and other security measures and to address the need for potential prohibitions or restrictions that should be imposed on the demonstration. The RG's work also includes general surveillance of political groups. They infiltrate organisations of all kinds in order to keep spontaneous demonstrations and 'direct actions' under police control.

A number of recent incidents have contributed to a rethinking of policing methods at public assemblies. One general principle is that demonstrators should never be 'trapped' or left without means of escape. The need for escape routes was made explicit when nine people were crushed to death against the railings of the Charonne metro station in 1960 following demonstrations related to the Algerian war. More recently the death in 1986 of a young Algerian as a result of a beating by a special police squad lead to debate on how much violence could be legally used in a riot situation. The two policemen involved in the killing were members of a special police unit created to respond to the presence of outside elements joining a demonstration for the sole purpose of stealing and rioting. The special squad followed people using motorbikes and arrested them away from the main body of the parade and away from the media. The policemen only received suspended sentences but the special force was subsequently dismantled.

Apart from batons, the police have access to tear gas and water cannon to control disorder at demonstrations. Use of rubber bullets was considered at one stage, but rejected because they were believed to be as dangerous as live ammunition when fired at close range. Heavier weapons or military equipment are sometimes used for technical reasons but have not been called on for other purposes since the anti-nuclear protests of the 1970s and 1980s.

While the police have a responsibility to facilitate legal demonstrations, they can also operate in such a way as to infringe the right to demonstrate. One such method is through failing to provide sufficient or effective policing. Act Up noted that on one of the first demonstrations that they organised, the police did nothing to divert traffic as they reached one of the major road junctions in Paris. The group challenged the police who were eventually forced to act on the matter and stop the traffic to allow the demonstration to pass. A smaller demonstration or a less determined group would probably have been unable to go any further and be prevented from completing their legal demonstration. Although the attitude of policemen could also sometimes be overtly hostile, in general aggressive attitudes were most likely to occur when events have not been planned properly and when the police were heavily outnumbered by demonstrators. A police force put in a vulnerable position is always more likely to resort to aggressive tactics and excessive use of force.

However, few groups complained about the behaviour of the police under normal circumstances and in the case of legal demonstrations most organisers felt that they had a good relationship with the police on the ground. The relationships that built up over time could work to the benefit of the authorities at times of tension. The presence of the *Renseignements Généraux* police is a regular feature of demonstrations; most officers were readily identifiable and known to demonstrators. These contacts often left them as natural intermediaries between the uniformed police and the demonstrators. At times of major strikes the role of the police authorities has gone beyond the usual policing duties as their relationship with diverse organisations has allowed them to open channels for discussion between government and the demonstrators. According to the *préfecture* this tactic has proved very successful and has greatly contributed to the peaceful resolution of conflicts in recent years.

Restricting Parades

The fact that the right to demonstrate is rarely restricted by a complete ban does not mean that the freedom is absolutely protected. On the contrary, the authorities can use many approaches to actually hinder the right to demonstrate. Most restrictions are justified by practicalities such as the number of demonstrations already taking place on a certain date, the need for a police presence in many different operations, etc. Concern for traffic can also limit, within moderation, the right to march through busy or strategically important streets.

According to the *préfecture* the banning of parades has not become an issue in France because alternatives are always offered. Even when a compromise on the time or the route might not seem available, groups can usually find a way around the restrictions. When the police trade union was prohibited from organising a demonstration in their own name another union organised an event in which only policemen took part. In a similar example, an anti-racist group organised demonstrations in solidarity with Kurdish people who had been refused the right to organise such events themselves.

If banning a demonstration is likely to attract more publicity than a small parade would have, it is sometimes more judicious to try to undermine the demonstration itself. One effective way of diluting the message expressed by the demonstrators is to ensure that another element will be prioritised in the news coverage. This has consistently been the case each time rioting has broken out at the end of a demonstration. A representative of one union explained that they had stopped organising rallies that were to end in the late afternoon as rioting regularly started after the main body of the marchers had dispersed just in time for the live eight o'clock news. The message of the demonstration would then be obscured by the violence of the rioters. In recent years a number of demonstrations have had to confront the problem of riotous elements infiltrating the march. This has been particularly detrimental for student demonstrations and several groups have accused the police of infiltrating demonstrations to stir up the rioting. Such methods have been used successfully in many countries, and this suggests that such accusations are more than simply a sign of paranoia, but rather describe a political technique that can be used more efficiently than prohibition to diminish the right to demonstrate.

Although banning a parade is a relatively rare occurrence, when it happens it does provoke debate. One problem is that the apparent lack of objective criteria to justify why, and when, a parade can be banned gives the impression that prohibitions are imposed for political reasons. Public order is a very vague notion and has different definitions depending on the political climate of the time. It is not a legal but a political concept. The jurisprudence clearly reveals that demonstrations by right-wing groups are more likely to be banned by left-wing authorities and vice-versa, this casts some doubt on the 'public order' justification (Turpin 1993). Most organisations felt that demonstrations were only banned if there was sufficient political will to do so and that some kind of compromise could always otherwise be found. Preventing a demonstration therefore seems to depend on the balance between political will and the number of people potentially mobilised by the demonstration. A million people on the street have an unconditional right to demonstrate since the policing costs to prevent them from gathering would be so high that the authorities would be unlikely to press for a ban.

Only one situation appears to lead to a systematic ban on demonstrations. Even though it is not mentioned in the legislation covering parades, being able to organise a demonstration to criticise the actions of a foreign regime depends entirely on the tacit approval of the government. Freedom of expression and freedom of assembly are readily suppressed when it comes to the visit of foreign dignitaries. It was widely accepted that demonstrating against a foreign president would not be possible on the day of his/her visit. As the *préfecture* explained, you would not want your neighbours to picket your house when they do not agree with your choice of guests. The issue is nonetheless a serious one. For example, demonstrations criticising the Turkish regime have been systematically banned. The authorities usually blame the potential terrorist connections of Kurdish refugees but others suspect that such restrictions had more to do with the importance of the arms trade than with any threat to public order caused by a group of less than fifty people. As a result groups often organise 'direct actions' and do not give notification of their intentions in order not to face a prohibition.

The question of the rights of foreigners to demonstrate is also worrying in terms of civil liberties and goes beyond the issue of diplomatic relations. Foreign visitors do not have a right to demonstrate, and their presence in demonstrations is only 'tolerated'. In practical terms, it means that French associations will often organise a demonstration in the name foreign groups. Furthermore, if non-nationals are arrested during an unauthorised demonstration or after the dispersion order has been given, they can be automatically expelled from the country. This has happened on several occasions and can only be avoided if a sufficient number of people react to stop the process and prevent the deportation. As a whole, the violence used to repress demonstrations organised by foreign groups, and the complete discretion left to the authorities when dealing with these situations, does not improve the broader culture of rights in the country.

In recent years a new phenomenon has emerged in France with the rise of the *Front National*. Most of the contentious demonstrations are now linked to the issue of racism. The 'democratic' solution of allowing both FN events and the counter-demonstration still prevails and according to the *préfecture* FN parades are very rarely banned, contrary to what the party would like people to believe. *Front National* officials however regularly accuse the government of discriminating against them and insist that their right to demonstrate has been violated on a regular basis. The banning of a *Front National* demonstration is nonetheless a difficult issue. Left wing groups regularly oppose the right of extreme right groupings to demonstrate. Some organisations boasted of having prevented 'fascist' assemblies from taking place by threatening to cause so much disruption with their counter-demonstration that the authorities had to ban both events. This raises the question of whether it is acceptable for one section of society to be allowed to decide what opinions deserve the right to be expressed. Seeing politically motivated restrictions on the right to demonstrate in a positive light can be short-sighted, since it creates a precedent that could always be used in a different way in a different political climate. If democratic ideals are fully respected, counter-demonstrators should be allowed to express their disagreement with the ideas defended by the members of the main demonstration, but that does not mean that they have a right to prevent them from expressing those ideas in the first place.

Conclusions

Demonstrating and protesting are important facets of French social and political life. The right to demonstrate is built into the broader legal framework and the boundaries have been established through practice. But such practice has also made it clear that there is no absolute right to demonstrate, rather demonstrators are expected to enter into a process of discussion and negotiation with the police authorities in order to establish appropriate terms and conditions for each public event.

When an agreement has been reached, it is set out in a form of contract, under which each party has different responsibilities. The organisers have a responsibility to ensure that their public event follows the terms and conditions while the police have a responsibility to ensure that the demonstrators are able to exercise their right to hold a peaceful demonstration. Protesters have no rights to prevent a legal demonstration from taking place.

This process of negotiation appears to work well with most groups and organisations; however, it is also clear that the ability to exercise the right to demonstrate can be affected by political considerations. Groups from both wings of the political spectrum have tried on occasions to prevent their opponents from holding demonstrations and meetings that they are opposed to. In such instances the police tend to play the numbers game, by facilitating both demonstration and counter demonstration where possible, but stopping both where necessary.

Furthermore, although France prides itself on its support for human rights, the government takes a pragmatic view in its readiness to prohibit demonstrations against visiting foreign dignitaries. In such cases the right to demonstrate is less important than the demands of foreign relations. However acknowledgement of such restrictions must be balanced by the seemingly relaxed way that the government responds to major protests by such groups as farmers and lorry drivers. Although they often cause immense disruption to everyday life, French citizens seem to regard such events as something to be tolerated rather than condemned. There is clearly therefore both a hierarchy of rights and at the same time an acknowledgement that no rights are absolute.

Italy

Processions, demonstrations and other forms of public assembly are significant events in Italian religious, cultural and political life. A wide range of demonstrations are held during the year. The state commemorates victory in the First World War in early November and the liberation from Nazi-Fascism in 1945 on 25 April; later, on 2 June, the establishment of the Italian Republic is celebrated. Various trade unions are involved in May Day parades each year (Donno 1990; Isnenghi 1997; Scoppola 1995). Besides these national events there are a range of more localised parades and demonstrations including commemorations organised by civil authorities; religious ceremonies and carnival parades; re-enactments of historic events; and a variety of social and political demonstrations that take place all over the country.

In Italy the right to parade is encompassed in the notion of freedom of assembly which is a basic constitutional right. Article 17 of the 1948 Constitution of the Italian Republic states that:

> Citizens have the right to gather peacefully and without arms. For meetings, including those held in a place open to the public, no prior notice is required. For meetings in public spaces prior notice must be given to the police authorities, who may forbid them only for valid reasons of security or public safety.

The concept of public order does not in fact appear in the Constitution but instead the notion of public safety is invoked in both articles 16 and 17. Threats to public safety are considered a necessary requirement for restricting the rights both to circulate freely and to gather peacefully. The notion of public safety has been quite clearly defined, it is linked to the need to ensure the prevention of violence while aiming at the maintenance of a peaceful coexistence for all sections of the community (Corso 1979; Fiore 1980). Any threat to a peaceful condition can be dealt with by preventing events that may contribute to its breach. The potential disturbance of public safety justifies measures that may be taken by the authorities to restrict the rights of citizens.

Legal Constraints

Although freedom of assembly is protected by the Constitution, it is however, subjected to restrictions in some way. Firstly, meetings must be peaceful and participants should not carry any form of weapons. Secondly, for meetings in public places prior notice must be given to the police authorities. For private meetings, or assemblies in places open to the public no prior notice is required.

Meetings can take both the form of *assembramenti*, that is occasional gatherings due to unexpected and unforeseen circumstances, and *dimostrazioni* which are gatherings that have a religious, civic or a political purpose. Further distinctions have been established on the basis of the location between private assemblies, assemblies open to the public and public assemblies. Private assemblies are gatherings that are held in private sites. Assemblies open to the public are held in places 'open to the public', this means premises or buildings to which access is allowed to members of the public at certain times or under certain conditions which are defined by the owners. Public assemblies are held in public places, which are understood to be any place where unrestricted access is allowed.

Further regulations to control public assemblies are set down in the legislation on public safety: the *Testo Unico delle Leggi di Pubblica Sicurezza*, known as TULPS (Single Text of the Laws of Public Safety). This law was established under the Royal Decree on Public Safety no. 773, and was originally introduced in 1931. Articles 18 to 27 of TULPS are concerned with the regulation of meetings in public places and with civic and religious processions.

TULPS was originally passed under the Fascist regime of Mussolini, but it has subsequently been refined through numerous judgements in the courts and some sections have been repealed. Furthermore the new Italian Constitution of 1948 has reversed the relationship between the power of the police authorities and freedom rights, and now the latter take priority over the former (Santosuosso 1988:185).

The basic requirement for holding a public assembly is to give three days notice to the authorities. The standard details that are required in the notice are the date, the time, the place and the route of the proposed event. The notification must also include details of the individuals responsible for the organisation and it must also include personal details of any speakers when speeches are to be held. The notice must be given in to the *questore*, the police superintendent in charge of the local province. The *questore* has the power to prohibit public assemblies but only for valid reasons of security or public safety. If the *questore* wishes to make changes to the organisers' plans, then he must notify them within 24 hours, but if he does not contact the organisers within this time, then they can legally assume that the demonstration can go ahead as planned. Thus the notification is not a request for permission, but is a communication that an assembly or a meeting is going to take place on a certain date, at a set time and along a specific route.

Policing Demonstrations.

The *questore* has responsibility to organise and co-ordinate the various police forces to control demonstrations. This can be a complex operation as there are five national police forces in Italy, two of which, the *Polizia di Stato* and *Carabinieri*, have responsibility for public order and public safety. The former is under the control of the Minister of the Interior, while the latter are controlled by the Ministry of Defence. Furthermore, use may also be made of the *Guardia di Finanza* if needs be as well as the *Polizia Municipale* which are under the control of the Mayor in each town. If trouble occurs as a result of a demonstration, then it is the *questore* who is held responsible and he can be removed from his post if necessary.

In the case of larger demonstrations where all of these forces might need to be deployed, the organisation of policing is carried out by a *Comitato Provinciale per l'Ordine Pubblico e la*

Sicurezza. This is a committee made up of the *questore*, a commander of *Carabinieri* and the *prefetto*, who is the local representative of the Minister of the Interior and who has overall authority to take all measures necessary to preserve law and order.

Negotiations and Agreements

Since the *questore* is responsible for public order and public safety he has the power to impose constraints on the time and place of demonstrations and he can impose a variety of restraints and restrictions. The *questore* also has the power to ban an assembly on grounds of concern for public health, public order or morality; this applies to religious ceremonies as well as to more overtly political events. In practice the *questore* always tries to reach an agreement over any restrictions he wishes to impose. Meetings are held between the various parties to try to accommodate different requests and in most cases compromises are reached.

If a prohibition or conditions are to be imposed, then the promoters must be notified of these in advance of the event. The organisers are entitled to lodge an appeal to the *Tribunale Amministrativo Regionale*, the administrative regional court, to try to have the decision overturned. The *questore* must give clear reasons for the restrictions being imposed, because by banning an assembly he can be seen to be imposing limitations on basic constitutional rights. Although the right to appeal remains as a legal safeguard, it is a time consuming process and could not be used to solve disputes in the short term, hence the reliance on negotiations.

Stewards

While the police have overall responsibility for public order, organisers of events are encouraged to deploy stewards both to control their own supporters and to ensure that any restrictions that have been imposed are complied with. Since the 1960s many of the trade unions have developed a more comprehensive stewarding system to reduce the need for police at their events. Although they have no formal training stewards are expected to ensure that the event is peaceful, orderly and legal and would normally be identified by badges or armbands. They are expected to protect the demonstrators from outside troublemakers and also from agent provocateurs who might be trying to stir up trouble from within the body of the demonstration.

If the promoters of a meeting fail to give notice, they are liable to a punishment of up to six months imprisonment and a fine up to L.800,000 (£300). It is not only people who are involved in the publicity and organisation of demonstrations who are considered as promoters, but this category also includes persons who have a more general involvement in its facilitation. This would include the people leading a demonstration and the stewards. However, individuals who address any such assembly are not liable to the same penalties. If an event is held even though a permit had been refused or conditions have been imposed by the authorities, persons who have contravened it, are punishable with up to one year's imprisonment and a fine of up to L.800,000 (£300). In this case those who address any such meeting are also liable to the same penalties.

Italian legislation does not operate a distinction between traditional or religious parades and political demonstrations. However, in practice there is obviously a clear difference between religious or civic processions that are held in rural towns or cities, which generate no opposition from any lobby or political group, and political rallies or meetings that involve one of the more radical groups. In the former instance permission for a parade can be given by the Mayor, who is responsible for public order in the absence of a local police station. Demonstrations or parades in a village or town are usually overseen by no more than a few members of the *Carabinieri* or *Polizia Municipale* who must always be present for public safety purposes.

In contrast, political demonstrations are often heavily policed by a variety of departments. In the case of political demonstrations a special police anti-riot squad, known as *reparto mobile*, is deployed and members of *Digos*, the political intelligence branch are also usually present. There are eight anti-riot police units across Italy, which receive specialised crowd control training. They may also be supported by other police forces, such as the *Carabinieri*. A variety of anti-riot equipment is available to the security forces, ranging from helmets, shields and truncheons to tear gas. Water cannons were used in the fifties. Rubber bullets are not used, and any attempts to introduce them have been rejected. Regulation firearms are always carried by police officers during demonstrations, in the past these have been widely and readily used against protesters.

Dispersing Gatherings

The police have a wide degree of discretionary powers to disperse gatherings both in public spaces and in places open to the public. Dispersion of an assembly can be carried out even if formal notification has been given and no ban has been imposed by the authorities. On the other hand failure to give notice to the authorities does not necessarily ensure a forcible break-up of a meeting by the police. Illegal gatherings can readily be dispersed but assemblies can also be dispersed when they are declared *radunate sediziose* (seditious assemblies). These consist of a gathering of at least ten people, which is deemed to be a threat to the peace. *Radunate sediziose* are declared when there is a degree of hostility against public authority or when the gathering is perceived to be about to disturb the peace.

For example, according to Article 22 of TULPS., a meeting would always be considered seditious if flags and emblems were carried which are symbols of social subversion, revolt or scorn towards the state, the government or the authorities. Demonstrators are also not allowed to wear forms of headgear that prevents them being identified. In practice, the police would tend to tolerate such infringements of the regulations in order to avoid confrontation or accusations by protesters that they acted in a way to restrict the right to freedom of expression, which is guaranteed by Article 21 of the Italian Constitution.

Once a demonstration has been declared unlawful it can be dispersed by force. In the first instance the police must ask demonstrators to disperse peacefully. If such an order is still ignored after three such requests have been given then the police may actively disperse the demonstrators. The order to disperse refers to all persons attending the assembly and it is not only restricted to participants. However, no violence should be used against people who are unable to leave the scene or against people who are on the ground. During demonstrations it is permitted to photograph both participants and police officers, but in the case of a crowd being dispersed photographers may be asked to leave the scene. However, any request to give film to the police forces is illegal. Finally, if excessive violence or abuse has been committed during the dispersal of a gathering, police officers may be subjected to an investigation by a magistrate and disciplinary measures.

Changes in the Policing of Protests

In the fifty years since the end of the Second World War the style of policing at parades and demonstrations has changed frequently and dramatically. Over this period Italy has been through various cycles of violence and repression as trade unions, left-wing parties and more radical groups have challenged the authority of the state. The state has often been accused of an over aggressive reaction to popular protests and at times it has been asserted that they have colluded with right-wing extremists to provoke trouble. Policing has been at the heart of this issue and the police have regularly been accused of being partisan and over violent. Ultimately widespread reform of the police was a necessary part of ensuring that demonstrations would pass off peacefully (della Porta 1995: 55-63).

During the late-forties and early-fifties there was severe repression of all forms of political assemblies and demonstrations. This reflected the policy of Italian post-war governments in marginalising the working class and left-wing parties and excluding them from political power. The police were a militarised body, which were trained to repress any threats to public order. They were given considerable latitude in the use of firearms against demonstrators. During this period almost one hundred people were killed by the police while taking part in demonstrations.

In the early 1960s government policy changed and a softer approach was taken to the handling of demonstrations, but the policy of restraint was reversed following the explosion of student demonstrations and widespread political protests in 1968. The police responded to violent protests with violence and widespread protests from all sections of the left and trade unions greeted the deaths of six demonstrators in 1968 and 1969. This led to a softening of police tactics and a more systematic process of bargaining between police leadership and movement leadership was established in order to try to reduce the frequent public violence. Nevertheless over aggressive police intervention and a cavalier use of batons, vehicles and tear gas led to the death of several protesters and even a number of passers-by. In addition, a widespread perception that the police were colluding with right wing groups undermined confidence in the security forces still further. The state strategy of dealing with political protests came to be known as the 'strategy of tension'. It was believed that the government was manipulating those on the political fringes to foment violence and thereby increase public support for more authoritarian policies.

In the second half of the seventies the state came under more sustained attack by a number of violent radical groups. During this period many of the radical groups, such as the *Autonomia Operaia*, refused to give notice of their demonstrations since they did not acknowledge the authority of the state. They would not engage in any form of communication with the authorities and were often ready to provoke a violent reaction from the police. Instead the two sides confronted each other on the streets. As a result prohibitions were frequently imposed against public gatherings and the police often intervened aggressively to break up demonstrations without discriminating between peaceful and militant demonstrators. Emergency laws were passed to fight the various terrorist groups who were challenging the state and although they were seen as repressive these laws were successful in constraining violent protests and support for the more militant groups.

By the eighties the state had largely defeated the threat of terrorism and as a consequence much of the emergency legislation was revised. Furthermore significant reforms of the police were introduced that led to the demilitarisation and professionalisation of the various forces. In part these were a result of pressures from within the police themselves who wanted a more democratic structure with the right to belong to trade unions. In part from a desire on behalf of the state for a higher quality of officers and in part it was a response to public concerns that the police were partisan and often over aggressive (Marinelli & Mazzei 1988). Demilitarisation, which involved making the police answerable to the Minister of the Interior, was particularly significant in changing police culture; while improved training was also reflected in changes to police practice.

One significant outcome was a more tolerant attitude toward protesting groups. Policing of demonstrations became much softer in style and more considered in its approach. Extra attention was paid to preventative intelligence gathering and potential troublemakers were more selectively targeted to ensure that demonstrations were able to pass off with a minimum of disruption. At the same time peaceful civil disobedience was more readily tolerated and as a result organisers of public assemblies were more willing to co-operate and collaborate with the police. This approach to the policing of demonstrations has continued to the present and as a result although there are still an extensive range of public gatherings and protests, violent conflict is not a major source of concern.

Recent Disputes

This new style of policing has now become more fully established and the policing of demonstrations have become more refined and focused. Many organisers feel that the police authorities now took a much more relaxed attitude to demonstrations, notification was accepted within the three-day time limit and any changes were normally subject to negotiation and discussion rather than simply being imposed. The police were also felt to be less assertive on the streets and were prepared to be flexible rather than sticking literally to the law.

However, political and legal disputes do still arise over demonstrations. The most significant recent case for legal purposes occurred in 1991 when a demonstration planned for Bolzano by the *Sudtiroler Schützen*, a pro-German speaking organisation, was countered by the neo-Fascist MSI who announced that they also intended to hold a protest meeting in the city on the same day. The *questore* decided that both demonstrations should be prohibited for fear of public disorder. The *Schützen* ignored the ban, held their demonstration and the organisers were subsequently prosecuted and fined. However, on appeal it was decided that the *questore* had been wrong to ban the demonstration by the *Schützen* and the conviction was overturned. The court asserted that the *questore* should have allowed the first demonstration of which he had been notified and restrict the second, which was the cause of potential disorder (Ruling 6812, 13 June 1994).

Further contentious demonstrations have resulted from political protests held by left-wing groups opposing meetings organised by extreme right-wings groups on the issue of racism towards immigrants or as a result of counter-demonstrations organised by supporters of *Alleanza Nazionale* (formerly MSI) against rallies by *Lega Nord* in support of their demand for secession from Italy. In general, following the previously cited case, the police are expected to facilitate the initial demonstration but they also try to ensure that the opponents have a right to protest. Nevertheless they also try to ensure that the two sides do not meet and may well call in extra riot police to ensure events pass peacefully.

Since the early nineties *Lega Nord* has become the strongest party in much of northern Italy and they have attempted to create new symbols and rituals that emphasise the distinctive historical and ethnic roots of the region which they have named Padania. Part of this process has been to hold parades and demonstrations to commemorate newly significant historical events. But the League has also begun to systematically challenge the authority and symbols of the Italian state by holding protests at various ceremonies and this has led them to make accusations of discrimination and a denial of their civil rights.

Lega Nord supporters recently demonstrated in the northern cities of Gorizia and Verona during official state ceremonies, and in Brescia, during an unofficial visit of President Scalfaro in September 1997. The demonstration in Brescia happened at a very tense time and the police were deployed to prevent *Lega Nord* supporters from entering the main square. However, tension arose and minor clashes occurred between opposing groups. *Lega Nord* subsequently complained about the inequality of treatment, because they had been restricted in their right to protest freely in the town while Padanian flags and emblems were banned from the square by the police. The League have also accused the authorities of manipulating counter-demonstrations so as to be able to restrict their events and of failing to protect them from their political opponents.

There is something of a contrast here. The state authorities, representatives of political parties and trade unionists all feel that changes in police culture and the reduction of social conflict are reflected in softer policing in recent years and a greater respect for the right of all sections to make their political opinions heard and seen. But the *Lega Nord* were more concerned with an apparent inequality of treatment and with restrictions which were being imposed by the central state on to the freedom of people to demonstrate against the state itself. In part this may be a result of their comparatively recent entry into national politics, which only dates from the late eighties, but in part it may indicate that the state still shows partiality to some sections of society. In the 1940s and 1950s it was the trade unionists that felt threatened, in 1960s and 1970s it was the radical left and in the 1990s it is the secessionists of the *Lega Nord*.

Conclusions

The right to peaceful assembly and the right to freedom of expression, which are protected by the Italian Constitution of 1948, have reduced the discretion of the authorities to impose restraints on parades and demonstrations. Over the years some parts of the public safety legislation (TULPS) have been declared unconstitutional by the courts, and although they are no longer used they have not been repealed.

Once notice has been given, the authorities can refuse to allow a demonstration on grounds of concern for public order, or they can place restrictions. In practice some form of accommodation is always sought and constraints on the route, the time or the style of the event are only imposed after discussions and agreement with the organisers.

Over the years the style of policing at demonstrations has changed considerably. A harsh and aggressive regime in the fifties, the early sixties and the seventies has given way to a much softer and tolerant handling of the demonstrations in the eighties and the early nineties. With social conflict at a lower level, a culture of mediation has prevailed.

Regarding confrontational demonstrations, the authorities have been required to protect demonstrations that have been duly notified. However, the right to protest at another gathering is also guaranteed, though no right is given to restrict the rights of others by breaking up or blocking the route of a legal demonstration. If this is the case police can intervene to avoid confrontation and to facilitate the legal meeting, but at the same time they are expected to guarantee freedom of expression to the other side. In practice restrictions can be imposed by police both to contain the situation or in order to reduce the possibility of public disorder.

Disputes involving some political parties and extremist organisations have recently occurred. Nonetheless, the authorities tend to maintain a selective attitude in their policing of the demonstrations. Thus a willingness to ban or disperse parades seems to depend on the political climate, both at local level and at national level. At the present time, football violence is the most serious public order issue to be managed by the authorities and it requires significant numbers of police to prevent public disorder when big matches take place.

United States
of
America

The New York St Patrick's Day parade is the oldest such event in the USA. The first parade was recorded in 1762 when Irish soldiers serving under King George marched through the commercial districts of the town. Organisation of the event was taken up by the Ancient Order of Hibernians two years after its formation in 1836, since when the Hibernians have continued to organise the annual event. The parade has flourished over the past one hundred and fifty years since that time and is the most prominent parade in America (Kelton 1985). The importance of freedom of assembly, of the right to parade, to protest and to demonstrate was recognised by the newly independent United States as a fundamental feature of a democratic society. These rights were set out and guaranteed to all in the First Amendment to the Constitution in 1791.

During the nineteenth century holding parades was an important facet of social life for many of the numerous ethnic and immigrant groups in America. The practice of parading was widely used to establish or consolidate communal identity, in displays of collective strength and to exert influence on local politics (Davis 1986). St Patrick's Day parades have been established extensively by the Irish community and the number of annual celebrations continues to grow. There are now over 200 such parades each year across the USA, some in communities with only the most tenuous of Irish connections. In many places the event has lost any political significance it might once have had and has become little more than a civic festival in which firemen and policemen march alongside high school bands and local traders. They are celebrations of local identity, rather than anything specifically Irish.

Nevertheless, holding parades and demonstrations remains a fundamental facet of American political life. Although the principle of the right to demonstrate was established under the Constitution, the limits of such rights and the ways and means by which they may be exercised in practice have been widely challenged through the courts. In the 1960s organising marches and demonstrations was a basic part of both the black civil rights and the anti-Vietnam war campaigns, while more recently neo-Nazi and Gay groups have sought to overturn restrictions imposed by the civil authorities by appealing to the Supreme Court.

Thus although demonstrating is accepted as a fundamental Constitutional right, interpreting how such rights are to be exercised in practice and determining where the limits of such rights lie has always been contingent on the wider political climate. The American ideal is in many ways an extremely liberal one. However, as long as some form of public assembly is allowed, there are still a number of practical constraints that can be imposed by the police or by local authorities to limit people's right to demonstrate how and where they want. The balance between competing rights may be tilted in favour of demonstrators, but rights are still contested and the tensions still remain.

Constitutional Rights

Freedom of assembly and the right to demonstrate are guaranteed under the First Amendment of the American Constitution. This states that

Congress shall make no law respecting an establishment of religion, or prohibiting the free exercise thereof; or abridging the freedom of speech, or of the press; or the right of the people peaceably to assemble, and to petition the Government for a redress of grievances.

In interpreting this Amendment the Supreme Court has been particularly concerned to ensure that the rights of dissenters, protesters and those that challenge the status quo are protected. As such, generalised legal prohibitions on forms of demonstration have been declared unconstitutional when challenged. The Court has argued that any abuse of the right of assembly should be dealt with by criminal prosecution rather than by prior restraint. Official control of any form of freedom of expression is viewed with suspicion, but at the same time freedom of expression must apply equally to all sections of society.

It has therefore been felt that there should be special protection for the rights of those who wish to be provocative or challenging to dominant or widely accepted ideas. Many of the key cases that have been fought through the courts have been aimed at extending the rights of expression and assembly and reducing the power of the authorities to impose restrictions. This has meant that the Courts have overturned restrictions on neo-Nazis marching through a Jewish suburb of Chicago, have protected the rights of the Klu Klux Klan to demonstrate and have affirmed that it is acceptable to deface or to burn the American flag as a political protest.

As a result of such judgements it is accepted that the government does not have the power to restrict forms of public expression simply because of the message, the ideas, the subject matter or the content that is being conveyed (Gora et al 1991:5-6). Nevertheless the authorities do have the power to restrict assemblies if they are likely to result in serious disruption to public order, the 'clear and present danger' test. In such cases the actions of the demonstrators must be both directed to inciting lawless action and likely to produce such action. The police can then control or disperse the demonstrators.

The right to demonstrate extends also to the right to counter-demonstrate, but does not extend to the right of a hostile audience to prevent or restrict the holding of a legal demonstration. Of particular significance is the understanding that a parade or demonstration should not be banned or rerouted or restricted in any way simply because it might cause offence to people either on the route or in the general area. Working from the belief that political expression will very often be provocative, the Court has determined that in such instances the police have a primary responsibility to protect the demonstrators from the hostile audience. While this has often meant that right wing and racist groups have been treated in a somewhat liberal manner, these arguments were also used in the 1960s by civil rights groups and anti-Vietnam War demonstrators to insist that their demonstrations should be protected.

The underlying principles were most clearly elaborated in a 1978 judgement known as the Skokie case. The National Socialist Party of America were effectively prevented from holding a march and rally through Skokie, a predominately Jewish suburb of Chicago, by the local authorities. The National Socialist Party appealed and the Supreme Court ruled that the restrictions were unconstitutional and the march and rally should be allowed. The Court stated that even though displays of the Swastika would be deeply offensive to many of the residents, this did not justify restricting the right of free speech (Gora et al 1991:81-2). Nevertheless although the Court determined that the neo-Nazi group had the right to hold their rally, this right was never actually exercised. A large crowd of protesters gathered in the town centre on the day of the proposed march and the rally was held at a non-contentious location.

This example therefore also illustrates something of the pragmatism that underlies the American system. Although the Skokie case is held as an example of the extent to which provocative protests are given legal sanction in America, less recognition is ever given to the fact that the group were unable to exercise their right to demonstrate because of the opposition that the proposed event generated. In such situations the police do have an obligation to protect legally held demonstrations, but in practice this is not always possible. In such cases the police ultimately have to make decisions based on concern for public order and they can not necessarily guarantee the safety of provocative demonstrators.

Practice

The underlying thrust of the numerous interpretations of the Constitutional implications of local laws, state laws and police decisions is that the Constitution demands that freedom of assembly should be protected and facilitated by the authorities if it is held in a peaceful manner and in a traditional public forum. A public forum is defined as property that is owned by the government and open to the public, in practice this normally means most streets, sidewalks and parks. However, even this is never such an unconstrained right as might be suggested.

> The privilege of a citizen of the United States to use the streets and parks for communication of views on national questions may be regulated in the interest of all; it is not absolute, but relative, and must be exercised in subordination to the general order (*Hague v CIO*, 307 US 496, 515-16, 1939).

Exercising the right to demonstrate therefore has to be balanced with the rights of other sections of the community, and public assemblies can be limited in some ways providing that the restrictions are 'content neutral', that is they are not imposed to censor the expression of ideas. As one member of the New York Police Department told us 'there is a Constitutional right to demonstrate and to protest, but there are still questions to be decided where this right ends and where the wider public rights begin'.

The Supreme Court has formulated a doctrine to guide such decision-making processes known as the 'time, place and manner doctrine'. This stipulates that while people have a right to demonstrate, the authorities have to be aware of the broader picture. They therefore do have the right to impose 'reasonable' restrictions on the 'time, place and manner' of such public events in order to prevent them from 'unreasonably interfering with nearby activities and individuals' (Gora et al 1991:165-6). Having the right to demonstrate does not mean that one has the right to demonstrate where one will, when one will or how one will without due regard for one's fellow citizens.

Policing

The police have a responsibility to facilitate public assemblies, except if there is a serious threat to public order, and are not allowed to impose restraints on the content of parades that might be interpreted as any kind of censorship. However, as we have seen, the 'time, place and manner' doctrine allows them some degree of flexibility over the form, the style and the scale of parades and demonstrations. Policing structures and legal systems can be very decentralised and localised in America (Brewer et al 1996) and therefore it can be difficult to make broad generalisations over the means of administrating and regulating public assemblies, however the need to obtain a permit for a demonstration is widespread.

In New York organisers are required apply to the appropriate department of the NYPD at least 36 hours in advance, but often longer notice is given to facilitate the police. Normally obtaining a permit is a formality, but the police check to see if there are any potential problems, such as other events around the same time, before one is issued. If there are any concerns, then they will negotiate with the organisers to try to reach an agreement before they issue a permit.

In Boston organisers must give at least 48 hours notice to the City Transportation Department in the Mayor's office. Requests for a permit are considered by representatives of the police, as well as those of the parks and transport authorities. As with New York, organisers would be expected to negotiate over any concerns the authorities might have, but at the same time the police felt that they were limited in their ability to restrict the right to demonstrate.

The most widespread concern that demonstrations give to the authorities is disruption that may be caused to the free flow of traffic or to commercial activities. Although some disruption is an expected product of the demonstration, the police try to minimise it. Parades therefore may be kept away from key locations, prohibited during rush hours or after dark, or restricted to the weekends. The New York Police Department maintains an informal prohibition on demonstrations past the United Nations building on First Avenue and an arbitrary limit of fifteen parades each year on the central thoroughfare of Fifth Avenue, although a number of others are held on adjacent streets. The overwhelming majority of parades in Manhattan are also restricted to weekends. Similarly the Boston Police Department has tried to restrict parades to the Downtown commercial heart of the city and prefers them to be held at the weekend. More recently they have had to respond to the concerns of local commercial and residential interests to limit the number of parades in this area.

Usually any proposed changes to the organiser's plans are subject to negotiation, but the police can in practice impose constraints if they so wish. Often the organisers accept such constraints since it is usually the demonstration itself which is important rather than the route that is to be taken or the timing of the event. However sometimes restrictions are considered unacceptable, in which case the organisers have three options. They can try to mount an illegal demonstration, they can postpone the event and continue negotiating, or they can accept the restrictions. Whichever option is taken they also have the right to appeal through the courts. However because of the time that the appeal procedure can take, several years if it goes to the Supreme Court, this does not resolve the initial problem.

In most disputed cases a compromise agreement is reached, but on occasion the demonstrators ignore the police restrictions and hold an illegal march or rally. In such cases the police claim that they would make a pragmatic response to the situation. If they could control the demonstrators, then they would do so; but if the greater threat to public order would be to confront an illegal demonstration, then they would facilitate the event while retaining control of the streets. This has happened recently in New York when dealing with some of the radical Gay groups who had been restricted from holding a parade past the main Roman Catholic cathedral on Fifth Avenue. When a number of demonstrators insisted they would march their preferred route and ignore the restrictions, the police accepted that it was better to allow an illegal march through Manhattan rather than try to prevent it and be confronted with large numbers of angry protesters (McCarthy and McPhail forthcoming).

The police argue that in such situations their aim is to control the situation with minimal recourse to an aggressive or violent response. Nevertheless they do have a variety of equipment that they use for crowd control. For most demonstrations officers would be dressed in standard uniform, riot police would be deployed nearby but out of sight, while heavy wooden barriers would be used to restrict movement and close off streets. Individual officers have helmets, masks, shields and batons and are equipped with small pepper sprays that are for use at close quarters. Sergeants also have access to a larger pepper spray that can be used to cover a wider area. Water canon and hoses are available, but have not been required in recent years. Plastic bullets are not used by the NYPD but when asked how they would react to being attacked by petrol bombs, a Task Force officer said without hesitation 'we would use live ammunition'.

Riot police have been brought in to control violent crowds on numerous occasions since the rise of mass demonstrations of the 1960s. However, the majority of such interventions have been in response to rioting that has resulted from more generalised political or racial tensions, rather than being sparked by a legal march or rally (McPhail et al forthcoming). Most demonstrations and protests have been peaceful.

Counter Demonstrations

The police have a similar responsibility to facilitate protests and counter demonstrations as they do towards other forms of freedom of assembly, although not to the extent that a counter demonstration could impede the original event. In the case of protests the police are guided by the doctrine of 'sight and sound'. This indicates that protesters should be permitted to hold their protest within sight and sound of the object of their protests. Again, as it is considered acceptable to use amplifiers at protest, this can be liberally interpreted to ensure that opposing groups are kept well apart.

In practice protests or counter demonstrations can be somewhat ritualised affairs at which both sides play by relatively formal and mutually acknowledged rules. In New York there has been an ongoing protest by the Irish Lesbian and Gay Group (ILGO) over the refusal by the AOH to allow them to take part in the St Patrick's Day parade. The ILGO protest in 1997 took place near to the starting point of the Hibernian parade early in the morning of St Patrick's Day. The protesters began by walking up and down with placards on the pavement but eventually a small group of about thirty five demonstrators broke through the police cordon and blocked Fifth Avenue. The police tried to persuade them to leave voluntarily but the demonstrators refused and about half sat down on the street. The police then moved in and systematically arrested all those involved and took them to the police station to be charged. Having made their point to the assembled media, the remaining demonstrators then dispersed.

The majority of the police at the scene, in normal uniform, were concerned with crowd control and the removal of the arrested persons, while members of the Task Force were available as back up but remained out of sight. However the policing operation was significantly more elaborate than it at first appeared for alongside the operational officers were two members of the Community Policing Unit. These officers wore different colour jackets and remained apart from operational matters, their rationale was that 'we will have to come back tomorrow and pick up the pieces' and therefore they had an interest in constraining the behaviour of the police as much as that of the protesters. The Community Police officers acted as intermediaries, keeping a line of communication open with the protesters, trying to influence their actions, letting them know what would happen if they broke the law and trying minimise the disruption they might cause. Significantly they were not under the control of the officer in charge of operations, but rather worked directly to the office of the Chief of Police. Therefore, although they might be relatively low ranking officers, if they felt the operation was being badly handled they could communicate their concerns immediately to the highest rank and suggest a change of strategy. In practice the Community Police officers worked with the officer in charge of operational matters to ensure the protest went as peacefully as possible.

As well as the involvement of the Community Police officers, the policing operation was also supervised by members of the NYPD Legal Department. The police lawyers were present to ensure that the operational officers complied with the letter of the law in breaking up the protest and in the manner in which they arrested the demonstrators. In some cases protesters also have legal representation at demonstrations; in such cases both sets of lawyers monitor the proceedings. As with the community police the police lawyers were outside of the normal command structure, and as civilians they could advise the officer commanding the operation without concern for differences of rank.

From the perspective of the police, the operation to control the ILGO protest went according to both schedule and plan. The protest was facilitated but was also dealt with smoothly. Thirty-five people were arrested for blocking the road, about half were released later that day while the remainder spent the night in jail. The parade itself was not disrupted and began on schedule shortly afterwards.

St Patrick's Day

The St Patrick's Day parades are the longest established and largest events in both Boston and New York. The Boston parade is a dual anniversary as it marks both St Patrick's Day and the local celebration of Evacuation Day, when troops loyal to the British crown abandoned the city to George Washington's forces in 1776. The City Council organised the celebrations until 1947 since when the parade has been run by the South Boston Allied War Veterans' Association.

As noted above the New York parade has been organised by the Ancient Order of Hibernians since 1838 and because of this longevity has a certain privileged status. The event is considered a 'grandfather' parade and as such has an almost sacred status, both in the city and among other St Patrick's Day parades. Nevertheless this has not prevented it from adapting to the changing geographical pattern of the city. Over the past one hundred and fifty years the route of the parade has varied regularly as the city has developed, although it has always tried to occupy the commercial heart of the city for the day. The parade has taken a linear route along Fifth Avenue since 1879 although the length of the route has been shortened at least twice since the 1950s (Kelton 1985:97).

The New York parade is always held on St Patrick's Day itself regardless of which day of the week it falls upon. Of the fifteen annual parades along Fifth Avenue the only other events allowed to disrupt the commercial life and traffic flow by being held on weekdays are the Columbus Day parade in October and the War Veterans' Council parade on 11 November. When in 1982 it was suggested that the St Patrick's Day parade should be moved to a weekend to avoid the disruption to business this provoked considerable opposition and the proposal was swiftly rejected (Kelton 1985:103).

In a similar fashion the pre-eminence of the New York parade has meant that it is the only such parade in the area that is held on the actual anniversary of St Patrick. The other forty-five St Patrick's Day parades held in New York State each year are held over the weekends preceding and following the anniversary, while the Boston parade is held on the Sunday nearest to March 17th. This means both that the smaller events can attract important figures from the AOH and the Irish community and good quality bands while at the same time the New York parade remains the most important parade. In fact this has led to problems for the AOH as more and more people and bands have wanted to parade through Manhattan and they have been forced to operate a waiting list system for new organisations who wish to take part in the parade. Even so it is felt that the parade has become too big as it now takes five hours to pass any one spot and ways are being considered to reduce the numbers of some groups.

Controlling Alcohol

Today the St Patrick's Day parades cause few problems for the police apart from concern for traffic flow, but in the 1970s the consumption of large amounts of alcohol meant that both the Boston and New York parades could become quite wild and even violent events. The organisers were concerned that the parades were losing their reputation as respectable family events and the police were concerned at the excessive drunkenness, street fighting and assaults on their officers.

In the early 1980s new regimes were introduced in both cities to prohibit drinking on the streets in the vicinity of the parade routes. These were preceded by big publicity campaigns warning people that drinking on the streets would no longer be acceptable and all alcohol would be confiscated. Bar owners were also warned of the new regime, while they were not required to close a close eye was kept on any near the route. Many bars now choose to close for the duration of the parade. In New York police officers are deployed for a few blocks surrounding the entire parade route and are empowered to remove alcohol from anyone trying to get to watch the parade. In Boston police accompany a rubbish truck which covers the entire route in advance of the procession and all alcohol is immediately put through the crusher.

Although it took two or three years to be effective, it is felt that the transformation in the nature of both parades has been dramatic. The police are largely happy with the drinking levels and even though over one thousand summons were issued in New York in 1997, feel that they are in control of the situation. The parade organisers are also happier and feel that they now have an event that is family orientated once again. Similar tactics have been applied to a range of other large parades and public celebrations. The police feel that as long as the ground is prepared in advance and people know what to expect, then they will encounter few problems in controlling alcohol consumption.

Conclusions

Although the right to march and to demonstrate was guaranteed under the United States Constitution over two hundred years ago, the limits of such rights have remained open to dispute and subject to re-interpretation. In recent decades the Supreme Court has addressed the issue on many occasions and has continued to deliver judgements that extend peoples rights and limit the powers of the authorities to restrict freedom of assembly. But it is also clear that the ability to exercise one's constitutional rights must be applied equally to all sections of the community. Neither the courts nor the police should discriminate against one group or in favour of another.

The longevity of the Boston and New York St Patrick's Day parades gives them a certain status as grandfathered events but more recently established communities have also established the right to demonstrate on the major thoroughfares of these cities. The Irish take control of Fifth Avenue on March 17, but they will be followed in the coming months by the Greeks, the Jews, the Puerto Ricans, the Germans and others. In asserting one's rights, one also has to acknowledge the rights of others.

Under the libertarian regime that has evolved in America, the right to demonstrate largely takes precedence over concerns for the sensibilities of those who might be offended or who would object to parades and their associated visual and oral expressions. A recent judgement made it clear that there was a direct and necessary relationship between a parade and the audience.

> We use the 'parade' to indicate marchers who are making some sort of collective point, not just to each other but to bystanders along the way. Indeed a parade's dependence on watchers is so extreme that ° if a parade or demonstration receives no media coverage, it may as well not have happened (*Hurley v Irish-American Gay Group of Boston*, 115S.Ct. 2338, 1993).

This argument also relates back to the points we made earlier about the relationship between a march and the audience. The Supreme Court has indicated that a hostile audience did not have a right to stop a demonstration, but in this judgement it is plain that while an audience may not want or need a parade, the parade always needs an audience, whether hostile or otherwise. As expressive and communicative events parades require an audience to have any meaning. In such situations where the right to demonstrate is given some degree of priority, parity can only be achieved if such principles are applied equally to all sections of society.

Canada

Parading has been a feature of Canadian political life since the first half of the nineteenth century when Protestant and Catholic emigrants from Ireland began to organise regular commemorations on the Twelfth of July and later on St Patrick's Day. Toronto was the heartland of the Orange Order in Canada, the Order exerted considerable influence in local politics and the Twelfth parades were large and impressive events (Kealey 1988). Today the Order is no longer the powerful institution it once was, but it still holds a number of local church parades each year and parades through the city centre on the Saturday nearest the Twelfth.

Nowadays many of Canada's varied ethnic communities also use parades to celebrate their cultural and political identity in the city and over four hundred parades are held each year in the Metropolitan Toronto area. Many of these are small localised church parades organised by diverse Roman Catholic and Orthodox communities but some, like the West Indian Caribana, have become major events which draw tens of thousands of people onto the streets.

In the nineteenth century violent clashes and rioting regularly followed both Orange and Green parades and celebrations, but such disturbances have long since ceased (Cottrell 1993; Kealey 1988; Toner 1989). In recent years parades and demonstrations have not been a major source of public order concerns. The right to freedom of assembly is guaranteed by the Canadian Constitution, and while there are disputes over matters of the 'time, place and manner' in which parades might take place these are normally resolved informally and peacefully.

Rights and Freedoms

The right to freedom of assembly is guaranteed under the Canadian Charter of Rights and Freedoms which is constituted as Part I of the Constitution Act of 1982 (Knopff & Morton 1992; Mandel 1994). The Charter sets out four Fundamental Freedoms, which apply to everyone.

> 1. Freedom of conscience and religion.
> 2. Freedom of thought, belief, opinion and expression.
> 3. Freedom of peaceful assembly.
> 4. Freedom of association.

These fundamental freedoms are deemed to be guaranteed 'subject only to such reasonable limits prescribed by law as can demonstrably justified in a free and democratic society' (S.1). However, the Constitutional limits of the freedom of assembly set out in the Charter have yet to be tested in the Supreme Court.

The police have a responsibility both for ensuring that the fundamental democratic freedoms are applied to all and also for maintaining public order. These potentially conflicting responsibilities might on occasion result in a restriction of basic freedoms, however a recent report argued:

> The police officer must take into account that his actions must at all times safeguard the fundamental rights guaranteed by the *Charter* and analogous principles of law found in the *Human Rights Code* and elsewhere (Estey 1996:180).

There is obviously a question mark over how possible it is to adhere to this ideal. While the police have the power to invoke concern for public order in order to restrict the right to parade, it is also clear that a balance must be maintained between the competing interest groups in any area. Despite localised concepts of traditionality (grandfathering), parade organisers have to adapt to changing social, political and economic circumstances. In practice organisers are usually ready to discuss points of contention with the relevant police department in order to reach accommodation and thereby avoid more serious disputes.

Policing Parades in Toronto

Organisers of parades must apply to the Police Services Board for a permit. This is usually no more than a formality and normally is readily adhered to, although some left-wing groups refuse to apply on principle. Parades that are held without a permit amount to only a small number of the total, and in general the police do not take any action against the organisers of such events.

Permits should be applied for at least twenty-one days in advance, but this is taken as a loose guide. The police are often notified of small parades only a few days in advance, while they feel that larger parades require at least five or six weeks to administer and organise. This is rarely a problem, as small parades require little policing, while the dates of the larger events are well known. The Orange Order told us that they notify the police of their plans for the coming year in January, well before the legal deadline.

Because the dates for the main events vary little and are well known, the police are often pro-active in planning for them. An officer from the Community Policing Support Unit is responsible for co-ordinating matters and where possible meets with parade organisers well in advance to ensure potential problems are sorted out early. This practice is maintained at the event itself: officers with experience in dealing with public events and crowd dynamics are used where possible and emphasis is given to keeping communication open with the organisers to ensure any problems are dealt with quickly.

In practice the police are able to impose a variety of constraints and restrictions on parades. These usually relate to the proposed route or to the time of the event. Most restrictions aim at maintaining a free flow of traffic and avoiding disruption to business activities - there is an underlying fear that businesses might sue if a parade could be seen as causing loss of trade. Parades are therefore kept to one side of the road and away from streetcar routes. Right turns are preferred in order to avoid crossing the flow of traffic but parades are not permitted to complete a square on their route because this could block off areas and 'freeze' commercial access.

Similarly the police prefer parades to take place on a Sunday because this causes less disruption, but they also accept that as the aim of many parades is to get publicity or media attention the organisers expect the parade to take place on a weekday.

Besides the obligation to facilitate the expression of fundamental rights, the police are concerned with the cost of policing the parades. All parades are expected to run according to schedule, and particularly to depart on time. This is so that the police can deploy officers both efficiently and economically and to minimise disruption to traffic. Furthermore, if the aim of the parade is to raise money, then the organisers are expected to pay for the costs of the policing.

One implication of these economic concerns is that the police encourage the parade organisers to accept as much responsibility for the event as is practical, thereby minimising the demand for police time and resources. The organisers are expected to notify residents and commercial interests of their plans, they are expected to provide identifiable marshals and they are encouraged (although not legally required) to take out insurance in order to cover themselves against unforeseen occurrences for which they might be sued.

Grandfathered Parades

About thirty five of the parades in Toronto, including the Twelfth, the Carabana, the St Patrick's Day parade, the Sikh Khalsa parade and the Santa Claus parade, are regarded as 'grandfathered'. This gives the organisers a prioritised right to hold their parade on a specific day. However it does not create a sense of total sanctity around the event, the route might still be changed and other conditions imposed if necessary. For example, the Carabana parade is one of the largest events in Toronto, but has also ebbed and flowed in scale since it began in 1967. Although violence has only occurred in one year (1985), the police have become increasingly concerned with the potential for disorder as tensions have increased between their officers and black people.

> Their principal concerns are public safety and ensuring the continuous movement of the parade. Their strategy is essentially one of containment, as the barriers along the parade route ... bear witness (Jackson 1992:138).

One of the results of the recent growth of the Caribana procession and the police concern with public order has been that the route of the parade has been changed on a number of occasions. Some of these have been quietly accepted by the organisers, while others have been the 'subject of heated negotiation' (Jackson 1992:140). Nevertheless in the end the police have been able to impose their preferred route on the parade. The event now finishes in a large park where the crowds are more easily controlled.

Similarly the Orange Order have changed the route of their Twelfth of July parade through Toronto over the years. Norman Ritchie, General Secretary of the Orange Order in Canada, said that when the organisation was at its peak, in the 1930s, the parade 'used to bring the city to a halt'. But as the membership has declined and aged and the influence of the Order declined so the route has changed. The parade is now held on the Saturday nearest the Twelfth, the route has been considerably shortened and there is no return parade.

The Order itself now sees the Twelfth as a family day out. It has no political overtones and a picnic has replaced the platform speeches of some years ago. The police now regard the Twelfth parade as a relatively small and unproblematic event, which needs few officers and poses little concern. It now survives as something of a contrast to the steadily growing Caribana celebrations, which generates growing problems with illegal beer sellers and excessive consumption of alcohol. The police try to restrict illegal sales and confiscate the alcohol but it remains a difficult issue each year.

Conclusions

The right to parade and demonstrate is guaranteed by the Canadian Constitution and this seems to be accepted with little contention. There have been no cases where parades organised by one ethnic group have been challenged by another ethnic group in recent years, or violent outbursts at any major events. However in part this seems to be because the police are able to exert a degree of control over the conditions in which a parade takes place and the organisers are expected to be responsive to the changing circumstances of the city.

The Gay Pride parade is a final example of the way in which parading has been addressed in Toronto. The police noted that in the early years the Gay Pride parade was often confrontational and disruptive. But over time the route has been changed, the organisers have toned down some of the excesses, while the police have begun to address the way in which their officers treated the participants. The event has been part of the process by which a Gay identity has become established as a legitimate part of the wider society, but the organisers have also had to be responsive to the concerns of the wider community. The police now regard the Gay Pride parade as a successful community event.

While the right to demonstrate is an important civil right, in practice it is not seen as having a priority over the rights of others. In particular, parades are not allowed to disrupt the commercial life of the city too much. They are allowed to take their place within the social fabric of the city but not to dominate the lives of others. As an extension, the various parades organised by the numerous ethnic communities are held either within the commercial centre or within specific residential areas. Parades have not been allowed to be used to stir ethnic conflict. Despite these apparent constraints on the freedom to assemble and parade, this has not become a contentious issue in Toronto.

Israel

Parades, demonstrations, protests and other forms of public assembly are a vibrant part of Israeli social, religious and political life. The state itself and the civil authorities organise a variety of such events to commemorate and celebrate key anniversaries related to its foundation in 1949. Holocaust Day, Independence Day and Remembrance Day which fall in late April or May are among the most prominent (Handelman 1990). Similarly both supporters and opponents of the government, whether zionist or non-zionist, right or left-wing, religious and secular, Jewish and Palestinian all use a range of public assemblies to mobilise opinion in support of their own arguments (Kaminer 1996; Nunn 1993).

The right of assembly is regarded as a basic right by the Israeli government. This has not always been unproblematic. The right of assembly has been refined and consolidated over recent decades through the practice of demonstrating and by a willingness to challenge the state definition of the limits to such rights through the courts. Even now it is not a right that is extended equally to all members of Israeli society. Israel is an ethnically divided society, the majority (82%) of the citizens of the State of Israel are Jewish, while a minority (18%) are Palestinian. It is widely accepted that the right to freedom of assembly has not been extended equally to Palestinian Israelis. This is beginning to be challenged by some groups.

The issue of the right to demonstrate is further complicated with regard to the West Bank and the Gaza Strip which have been occupied by Israeli forces since 1967. The Occupied Territories are subject to military rather than civilian law, and under this system there is no legal right to freedom of assembly. Nevertheless, demonstrating remains an important part of political practice, for both Jews and Palestinians, but a practice that is continually subject to the dictates of power rather than principles of respect for human rights (B'Tselem 1992).

Finally, one should note that since 1994, a number of urban areas within the West Bank and Gaza Strip have come under the control of the Palestinian Authority. In theory the PA has guaranteed freedom of assembly to the Palestinian population, but in practice this has been a problematic area. The right to demonstrate for opponents of the PA regime or of PA policy has become increasingly subject to police control and restriction and is a source of concern for human rights groups (Mari 1997; LAW 1996).

While noting the importance of the freedom of assembly as a political and human rights issue within the West Bank and Gaza Strip, we feel that it is more useful to focus on the rights to assembly within the civil state of Israel, rather than areas of military control.

Freedom of Assembly

In Israel the right to demonstrate is regarded as a fundamental right of any democratic society. Until 1979 the police had considerable power to decide how such rights should be exercised and whether demonstrations should be allowed or banned. The courts had been unwilling to question police decisions and any requests for a judicial review 'met with a cool reception. The Court simply bowed to police discretion in matters of public order', the implications of the impact of such decisions for civil rights not being taken into consideration (Kretzmer 1984:65). This changed in 1980 when the Supreme Court made a substantive review of the issue in the process of overturning a police decision to refuse a permit for a demonstration. The limits to the right to demonstrate and the power to constrain freedom of assembly have subsequently been defined through key legal judgements and these have in turn been clarified in a series of directives issued by the Attorney General.

Permits

The basic requirements for those organising a demonstration, set down in the Police Ordinance, 1971 and the Penal Law of 1977, are simple. No prior notification is required for demonstrations that do not involve speeches or a march, nor are permits required for marches involving less than fifty people. But any demonstration that includes speeches or marches and is likely to attract more than fifty people requires a permit. Organisers of demonstrations must apply for a permit five days in advance to the District Commander of Police.

The police can refuse a permit on grounds of concern for public order, or they can place restrictions on the 'time, place and manner' of a demonstration. Often such constraints on the route, the time or the style of the event are imposed following discussions and agreement with the organisers.

If an event is held, even though no permit has been applied for, or after a permit had been refused, or if the conditions that have been imposed are ignored, then the demonstration is regarded as illegal. In such a case all those participating, not just the organisers, are breaking the law. The police can either arrest people or simply try to disperse the gathering.

If the police refuse to issue a permit, then the organisers can appeal to the Supreme Court to have the decision overturned. For such an appeal system to be operable, it requires the police to make their decision in advance of the day of the demonstration, however this is not specified anywhere.

Judicial Reviews

As Israel has no Bill of Rights, nor any law which clearly states that there is a Constitutional right to demonstrate, it has been left to the Supreme Court to establish the legal principle and limits of such rights (Kretzmer 1984). The most significant case has been *Sa'ar v Minister of Interior and Police* (1980). In the judgement Justice Barak confirmed that the 'freedom of assembly and procession' was a fundamental right which was recognised by Israeli law. But the judgement also went further by situating the right to demonstrate within the context of the rights of the wider community when the judge declared that people had a right to use the public streets for parades and demonstrations as much as for traffic and passage.

Just as my right to demonstrate in the street of a city is restricted by the right of my fellow to free passage in that same street, his right of passage in the street of a city is restricted by my right to hold a meeting or procession. The highways and streets were meant for walking and driving, but this is not their only purpose. They were also meant for processions, parades, funerals and such events (Quoted in Kretzmer 1984:66).

Parading and demonstrating were not therefore to be seen as something divorced or separate from the routines of daily social life, but were to be regarded as an integral part of them. Justice Barak asserted that granting a permit was not giving a favour but allowing someone to exercise a basic right. The judgement went on the make it clear that it was the duty of the police to enable people to exercise the right to demonstrate as much as it was their responsibility to facilitate other urban activities. The disruption caused by a demonstration was as much a factor of modern life as the disruption caused by traffic or by people shopping. It was the responsibility of the police to balance the competing demands on urban space.

Directives

As a result of another legal challenge to restrictions that the police had imposed on a demonstration (*Levi v Southern District Police Commander*, 1984), the Attorney General issued the *Directives on the Matter of the Freedom to Demonstrate*. These re-affirmed the state's acceptance of the basic right to demonstrate and clarified the nature and range of police powers to intercede in such cases (Heymann 1992:78-91).

The Directives state that the police should take into consideration concerns for public order, but noted that 'mere apprehension that a demonstration might lead to participants rioting or to actual harm to public safety or public order is not in itself sufficient to deny a licence'. Instead they asserted that more concrete evidence is required to justify such concerns, such as information of plans to violate public order or to incite violence, before the police can stop a demonstration.

The Directives also state that the police can not refuse a permit simply because of undue demands being made on police resources; nor because of disruption to urban routines that a demonstration might cause; nor because of an objection to the ideology of the demonstrators or the views that might be expressed. Furthermore, the Directives state that the police have a duty to protect people's right to demonstrate in the face of a hostile audience, regardless of the message that is being conveyed or of the demands that might be made on police resources.

Any assault directed at a demonstration by persons opposed to it, whether an assault based on political or social outlook, or an act of mere hooliganism, injures freedom of expression, which is one of the foundations of a democratic regime ... In so far as possible, the police must prevent such disturbances, and where they have occurred, must bring the suspects to trial (Heymann: 1992 85)

The right to demonstrate therefore extends to the right to protest at another demonstration, but it does not include the right to restrict other people's rights by breaking up or blocking the route of a legal demonstration. In such cases the police are expected to protect the legal demonstration.

While the police must facilitate the freedom of expression, they can still impose a range of constraints on a legal demonstration in order to reduce tension or if there is a fear of violence. Again there is a need to retain some degree of balance between protecting the right to freedom of expression and restricting that right if it might provoke or be designed to provoke violence. In such cases discretion is left with the police. The directives give the example of an assembly whose purpose is to demonstrate against religious values that could give fear of a breach of the peace if it was held in a 'clearly religious neighbourhood'. In such cases the right to demonstrate is not without limits and the police can impose specific restrictions.

> For instance, if the fear of the disturbance of the peace stems mainly from a specific placard, the police can demand that the placard not be used. If the fear stems from holding the demonstration at a certain place, the police can demand that the demonstrators move to a different place, as close as possible, in order to prevent the fear of disturbing the peace (Heymann 1992: 88).

While there is an opportunity to appeal the refusal of a permit, the imposition of restrictions based on concerns for public safety can be imposed at the time of the demonstration and in response to the actual conditions on the streets. Consequently when such decisions are made by the police there is no chance of an independent review of their judgement.

However, one should note that this directive focuses on those cases where the demonstration is deliberately provocative and likely to cause a disturbance, it does not mean that the police should necessarily restrict rights of assembly in response to a hostile audience. There is therefore a balance that needs to be maintained between demonstrations which aim to provoke a violent response, and which can be controlled, and those in which the violent response is disproportionate, and where the hostile audience should be controlled.

The types of constraint that can be imposed are similar to the restrictions that the American police can impose on the 'time, place and manner' in which a demonstration is held. The location or route can be restricted, banners or placards can be subject to control, the numbers participating can be limited and the timing can be changed or tightly defined. These indicate that despite its importance for a democratic society, the right to freedom of assembly and expression is never unlimited. It is always in some way balanced by the rights of other members of society and a need to acknowledge some responsibility to that wider society. One might therefore be expected to restrict (or have restricted) one's rights in some circumstances. The problem is to decide when restrictions are reasonable and when they are too great an infringement on one's liberty.

The aims of the directives and the attitudes of the courts appear to aim to consolidate and underpin the right of people to demonstrate and to engage in peaceful assembly. To an extent this was born out by the experience of people who organised or took part in these events. However it was also felt that these rights were not readily extended equally to all Israeli citizens, in particular Palestinian Israelis do not have the same opportunities to engage in freedom of assembly as do Jewish Israelis.

Demonstrating in Israel

In general people felt that the right of assembly was more clearly defined than it had been in the 1970s. This had been achieved by a combination of factors. Members of some of the more radical groups insisted that it had been important that they had set the agenda for the debate by constantly challenging the limits to civil rights as they had been defined by the state. This had been an important factor in extending people's right to demonstrate. It was seen as necessary that people had been willing to be arrested and go to court to demand their rights and to clarify the legal position. This had been supported by the work of Association for Civil Rights in Israel (ACRI) in challenging police constraints and in the willingness of the Supreme Court to overturn police decisions. The court had come to be regarded as a positive bulwark to any police tendency to restrict civil rights for fear of disturbance or disruption and it was also seen as an effective appeal mechanism.

Each of the Jewish groups said that they always applied for permits and always got them. However they accepted that some restrictions were liable to be imposed on such issues as the 'time, place or manner' of the demonstration, but that this was a matter for negotiation. There were no significant or 'traditional' routes for parades or demonstrations and therefore the route to be taken and the timing of a parade were obvious subjects for restrictions. Nevertheless such restrictions were not always passively accepted: in 1983 a court case had confirmed that it was acceptable to demonstrate near the Prime Minister's residence despite initial police attempts to restrict such activities.

It was also acknowledged that the police had accepted the court's rulings and worked within them to ensure that people's rights were upheld. However it was also noted that it was often more problematic when dealing with junior officers who were not so familiar with the law regarding civil rights. In contrast more senior officers were regarded as more liberal in their interpretations and it was often possible to reach an accommodation with them over controversial issues in situ.

It was also acknowledged that the police were now more aware of their responsibility to defend the rights of demonstrators, even if this required large numbers of officers and even if the demonstration was liable to offend people. Most left wing or peace demonstrations would expect to attract opposition from right-wing groups. But most groups stated that they would expect the police to protect their events from such opposing protests whereas in the past a hostile audience might have been used as an excuse to ban or restrict a demonstration. This was even the case when the demonstration was deliberately provocative: at least two demonstrations organised by the radical Hebron Solidarity Committee deliberately utilised Jewish religious symbols in a mock wedding and a mock funeral in a way that was expected to anger many passers-by. Nevertheless the police protected the demonstration and then provided a safe escort away from the area at the end for the demonstrators.

It was felt that right wing and religious groups were more assertive in demanding their rights, regardless of the legality, the disruption that might be caused or how this might impinge on the rights of other. However constraints were still placed on such demonstrations. Attempts by right-wing groups, such as Kach, to parade through predominately Palestinian areas had been stopped because they were seen as too provocative and liable to lead to a breach of the peace. Similarly, attempts by Jewish religious groups to gain access to the courtyard of the Temple Mount Mosque in order to pray have been stopped by police and the court has upheld their decision.

It was claimed that right-wing groups were less concerned about applying for permits, were more violent and aggressive in their demonstrations and that the police would allow such groups to cause more disruption than was justifiable rather than confront them. For instance, on May 6 1997 right-wing demonstrators blocked the main Jerusalem to Tel Aviv road as part of a protest. The police were eventually able to persuade them to move on but took no other action. It was felt that they would not have been so tolerant with a left-wing group. However it was acknowledged that if such groups became openly confrontational then the police would physically confront the demonstrators, and often in a very aggressive manner.

In fact the issue of police violence at demonstrations was a more general cause for concern. Police violence became a factor if the law was broken, if restrictions were ignored, when the police were trying to disperse or control demonstrators and when trying to control violent protesters. A representative of ACRI noted that they had received a number of complaints about police violence by demonstrators who opposed the Oslo Agreement, which framed the peace process between Israel and the Palestinians. The police have access to a variety of weapons ranging from batons to water hoses and teargas. In the West Bank they also used rubber bullets and live ammunition, but these were never used when dealing with Jewish demonstrators.

Palestinian Demonstrations

While acknowledging all these factors, it was also widely agreed that these applied principally to Jewish demonstrations and that other factors came into play if Palestinians were involved. One also needs to differentiate between joint Israeli-Palestinian demonstrations in Jerusalem and demonstrations by Palestinians elsewhere in the country.

The capital city Jerusalem is a divided and segregated city; East Jerusalem was part of the West Bank and Palestinian, while West Jerusalem is Israeli. Most Palestinians in Jerusalem are not citizens of Israel. In contrast Palestinians in the north of Israel, in the Galilee, and in the south, in the Negev, are Israeli citizens. Theoretically they have the same rights as Jewish Israelis, but in practice they are treated differently.

In most cases demonstrations in Jerusalem which involve Palestinians are organised in conjunction with Jewish left-wing groups. The Jewish group would 'organise' the event and apply for the permit that would probably be refused for a Palestinian demonstration, particularly if it wanted to enter West Jerusalem. Even so the police response to the demonstration on the day would depend on the proportion of Palestinians present. It was accepted that the police treated Palestinian demonstrations, or demonstrations with a large number of Palestinians harder than Jewish ones, while a higher proportion of Jews would temper police behaviour. In 1993 a demonstration protesting the mass deportation of Palestinians was given a permit, but when the police saw that the demonstration was largely Palestinian, and mainly Islamicists, their attitudes changed. They imposed a number of minor restrictions and reacted harshly to minor infractions and any unexpected events. At other demonstrations problems have arisen whenever Palestinian flags are carried or unfurled. If the police attempt to remove them, then violence is likely to break out and this can then lead to more widespread trouble and rioting. This is one area where being deliberately provocative is not accepted within the framework of civil rights in Israel.

There have also been problems over the location and route of joint demonstrations. Non-Israeli Palestinians do not have right of entry into Israel and public order problems would be likely to arise at such demonstrations within West Jerusalem. Joint demonstrations therefore usually begin in East Jerusalem but this can create problems for police security. In June 1997 a plan by Bat Shalom, a women's group, to assemble a joint demonstration at the Damascus Gate, on the boundary of East and West Jerusalem, was refused by the police because they feared that they might be attacked. Although it was felt that it had become easier for Palestinians to demonstrate in Jerusalem since the late 1970s, it was claimed that this has only been achieved by constant challenges to police restrictions.

A similar argument was made over the rights of Palestinian Israeli groups to demonstrate elsewhere in Israel. It was felt that the attitude of the police would depend on the nature of the demonstration and the demands that were being made. Many protests and assemblies focus on the issue of land rights and confiscations by the state, or on the building of new settlements. In the past if there was only a small number of people involved then land rights demonstrations were simply stopped or confronted by the security forces. Recently more restraint has been shown towards demonstrations in the Galilee and a greater willingness to allow them to take place, however less tolerance is shown to protests by the Bedouin in the Negev where demonstrations are quickly broken up.

The main Palestinian commemorative event has been Land Day (March 30) which marks the anniversary of land confiscations in 1948 and 1967. The day is usually marked by a general strike, and by marches, rallies and meetings. These have often ended in violence when the security forces try to disperse people at the end of the day. In recent years Land Day demonstrations have become more widespread. They are now held in both Israel and on the West Bank and have also been used to protest at opposition to expansion of Jewish settlements on the West Bank. More recently Palestinians have also begun to hold their own demonstrations to mark Israeli Independence Day. This is done by returning to their native villages, which are often now deserted, for a reunion and more informal gathering. Whereas people would usually comply with the law and apply for permits for Land Day demonstrations, this is rarely done for Independence Day gatherings. To date the police have not interpreted these as illegal assemblies.

So far Palestinian Israeli groups have not sought to challenge police restrictions through legal means nor tried to establish the limits of their own rights to demonstrate in the Supreme Court. The system is regarded as a Jewish system and therefore not responsive to the demands of Palestinians. However, at least one Palestinian human rights group is looking to push the case for Palestinian rights through the legal system and thereby extend those rights.

Conclusions

The right to freedom of assembly is regarded as a fundamental democratic right in Israel. The principle has been upheld by the Supreme Court, which has also elaborated on the balance that should be maintained between competing interests and rights. Directives issued by the Attorney General have clarified many of the practical matters arising from the landmark judgements. The police still have the power to refuse permits for demonstrations, but there is also an effective appeals mechanism through the Supreme Court against any restraints that they might impose. This mechanism is recognised by organisers of public events as being both fair and accessible and not a process that need delay a planned demonstration.

These processes are not static but have evolved over the past two decades, often as a result of pressure from the organisers of political events who have sought to take the initiative in extending the limits of civil liberties. However, such rights are still applied unequally within Israel. Palestinian Arab citizens of the state do not have the same right in practice to freedom of assembly as do Jewish Israelis. This is widely acknowledged among Jewish political activists and civil libertarians as well as by Palestinians.

In Jerusalem many Jewish groups have sought to facilitate Palestinian rights by organising joint demonstrations, and in the predominately Palestinian area of the Galilee local groups have become more assertive of their right to demonstrate. Although the two communities still do not have equal rights in this area it is felt that here too the Israeli State has become more responsive to the demands of Palestinians. The police and security forces have been less insistent on stopping or breaking up demonstrations in recent years. The next stage would be to take a case through the legal system and clarify whether the general principles and directives should apply to all Israeli citizens, of all ethnic groups and all political opinions.

South Africa

Under the apartheid regime non-whites had no rights to public assembly in South Africa and between 1976 and 1991 there was a blanket ban on all open-air gatherings. Nevertheless demonstrations and protests by the black community were widespread and frequently ended in violent confrontation with the South African Police Force. Street disturbances, and political violence more generally, increased in frequency from the late 1980s onwards as moves to reform the political system gained momentum. In response the National Party government established a commission of inquiry to look into ways of dealing with the political violence. One sub-committee focused specifically on violence at demonstrations and in its report made wide-ranging suggestions as to the changes that were needed to the system of organising and policing such public events. Many of its recommendations were included into the new law regulating public gatherings that came into force in November 1996. Besides the new law, a number of attempts were made to control the violence by making changes to the practice of managing demonstrations; these included setting up systems of independent monitors and reducing the role and impact of the riot police. The subsequent transformation of the political system following the multi-party elections in 1994; the adoption of a new constitution and the reform of the police force all had further impact on levels of political violence. During 1997 violence at demonstrations was not an issue of major public concern.

Demonstrations and Violence

Demonstrations, marches, rallies and other forms of public gatherings such as commemorations, celebrations, funerals and protests have been a prominent feature of black political expression in South Africa for many years. Official statistics do not reveal anything like an accurate picture of the total number of such events. Anthea Jeffrey notes that statistics gathered from press reports suggest that there were only 273 marches and gatherings held in the period 1970-1980, but she considers that this represents only a small percentage of the total. Her argument is supported by police statistics that reveal that there were nearly 11,000 gatherings in the nineteen-month period from January 1990 to July 1991 (Jeffrey 1991:33). Black rallies and demonstrations were informally permitted from 1989 onwards, and although they were still technically illegal, in most cases the legal formalities were ignored. Of the eleven thousand gatherings in 1990-91 only 1360 had been authorised, a further seventy had requested permission but had been prohibited, 851 were planned but did not request permission while the remaining 8608 were 'spontaneous' and lacked permission. Thus the vast majority were illegal gatherings.

The police response to such events was often violent and sometimes deadly. In March 1960 69 people were killed and 180 wounded at a protest against the pass laws in Sharpeville and three weeks later another two people were killed and 26 wounded at a similar protest in Langa. During the Soweto uprising of 1976-77 over 700 people were killed, many at protests and demonstrations; while in 1984 twenty people were killed and 23 injured when violence broke out at a funeral march in Uitenhage (Jeffrey 1991:25-29). Most of the gatherings in this period were in response to localised political dynamics (Mayekiso 1996), but the violence at demonstrations also generated their own dynamic as state violence in turn became a subject of commemoration and protest. The anniversary of the Sharpeville killings (21 March) and Soweto Day (16 June) both became annual occasions for large numbers of public gatherings and demonstrations.

In the period from 1990 to 1991 most of the illegal gatherings were dispersed without major incident. However police recourse to live ammunition did result in death and serious injury at Sebokeng (five dead, 161 wounded) in March 1990; at Johannesburg (2 dead, 10 wounded) in November 1990; at Daveytown (12 dead, 27 wounded) in March 1991 and at Ventersdorp (3 dead and 42 wounded) in August 1991 (Jeffrey 1991:35-40). Many lesser incidents resulting in the use of teargas, rubber bullets and live ammunition to disperse demonstrators received little publicity (Cawthra 1993:131-5). The violence at demonstrations was only part of more widespread political violence involving the ANC, the Inkatha Freedom Party, various Afrikaner groups and the police which left 4783 people, including 125 police officers, dead in the same two year period (Heymann 1992:4).

The period of transition from apartheid to a democratically elected government between 1990 and 1994 was marked by an escalation of public violence. Two of the key issues were the ongoing conflict between the ANC and the Inkatha Freedom Party over representation of the black community and local control of territory, and the continuing antagonism between the black political movements and the South African Police Force (Brogden and Shearing 1993). One major attempt to address this problem was through the National Peace Accord that was drawn up in 1991 and signed by all the main political parties (Cawthra 1993, COMSA 1993, Shaw 1997). The Accord aimed to set out a series of general principles defining the fundamental democratic rights and responsibilities that would form the basis of the new South Africa and which signatories were expected to strive to uphold. It also established Codes of Conduct for both political parties and the police relating to their attitudes and responses to public violence.

But the Peace Accord also went further by proposing a range of practical initiatives through which the violence might be countered in the period prior to the elections. The two most prominent initiatives were the formation of a Commission of Inquiry Regarding the Prevention of Public Violence and Intimidation, which became known as the Goldstone Commission after its chairman Judge Richard J Goldstone, and provisions for a National Peace Secretariat along with a number of Regional and Local Dispute Resolution Committees.

Goldstone Commission

The Goldstone Commission was charged with the responsibility of inquiring into the phenomenon of public violence and intimidation in South Africa and to attempt to identify the causes of such violence and the people involved. It was also expected to make recommendations to the State President as to how such actions might be reduced or stopped. The Commission's remit was extremely wide ranging but one specific area that it focused on was the issue of violence at demonstrations. To address this problem the Commission constituted a multinational panel of experts from the USA, Canada, UK,

Belgium and the Netherlands to review law and practice in a range of countries and to make recommendations as to the way forward for South Africa.

Many of the suggestions and recommendations by the international panel were subsequently incorporated into the new legislation covering the holding of public assemblies, the Regulations of Gatherings Act, which is reviewed below. Nevertheless it is worth considering some of the general points made in their report *Towards Peaceful Protest in South Africa* (Heymann 1992). This begins by setting out the basic general principle which underpins its thinking and eventual recommendations:

> The right to demonstrate is as fundamental a right of democratic citizenship as the right to take part in political campaigns. Where the purpose of demonstration is protest, the demonstration is at the core of free expression in a democracy. One of the central responsibilities of the police is to facilitate the right to demonstrate (Heymann 1992:ix).

The report proposes that these basic democratic rights can best be guaranteed by ensuring that the responsibility for peaceful public gatherings is shared as widely as possible. In their view this means that the organisers of the event, the local civil authorities and the police are jointly responsible for the events that they take part in, this is what the report terms the 'safety triangle' (1992:ix). The success of the safety triangle requires planning and co-ordination between the three parties and an acceptance and willingness to negotiate and compromise over any areas of dispute. However, in cases of more serious dispute the parties should have recourse to the Supreme Court to offer an independent judgement.

The authors suggest that 'to the maximum extent possible' the organisers of the event should be responsible for controlling the participants, while the civil authorities and the police should aim to facilitate the demonstration while at the same time minimising any inconvenience to other citizens. Again they recommend that reconciliation of disputes between demonstrators and other members of society or in the vicinity of the proposed gathering 'should be accomplished by negotiation and embodied in a binding understanding' (1992:9).

The report recommends that the organisers of all demonstrations should be required to give notification to the authorities. But the authors argue that as this does not involve seeking permission it serves to underline the fact that a fundamental right to demonstrate does exist. The report also recommends that there needs to be flexibility over the implementation of this aspect of the law and control of crowds by the police. It therefore suggests that failure to provide notification should not necessarily result in the dispersal of demonstrators, rather sanctions could be imposed on those responsible at a later date.

They also acknowledge that while all demonstrations will cause some disruption to others there are limits to the acceptable disruption. Furthermore, balancing the rights of different interest groups is a political issue and not merely a policing issue and should be dealt with as such by the political authority rather than the police (1992:11). While urging that such matters be considered as political issues the authors of the report are also concerned that decisions over political rights might in some instances be subject to political bias. Therefore there needs to be a means of independent arbitration through the courts in the last instance.

The report acknowledges, notwithstanding the fundamental nature of the right to demonstrate, that it is legitimate to impose some constraints and restrictions on demonstrators. In particular they were concerned with the balance between exercising one's rights and causing disruption to the rights of others or creating a threat to public order. However they did not feel that it was legitimate to deny a group the right to demonstrate on the grounds that they might be attacked by political opponents. They felt that the authorities had a responsibility to protect all demonstrations and that this principle held even when the demonstrators sought to deliberately provoke opponents or even to march peacefully through a hostile area. But again in the last instance they note that 'this right can be limited when the police are simply unable to provide reasonable assurances of safety' (1992:19). In other words the police should have the power to ban or restrict a demonstration if they believed this was the only means of preventing violent clashes.

The report also considered the role and responsibilities of the police in the peaceful facilitation of demonstrations. In particular they focused on the general need for good organisation and for the appropriate training and equipment for officers charged with crowd control. It recommended that the police needed to improve their skills in crowd management, in communication and negotiation and in the appropriate use of force. This they felt required considerably more sensitivity and restraint than had been exercised in the past.

Many of the reforms to the structure of the control of demonstrations, to the law and to the system of policing such events have been or are in the process of being implemented.

Monitoring Demonstrations

One relatively successful approach that was taken to try to reduce the tensions and persistent clashes at demonstrations and gatherings was through the use of independent monitors who attended public events to act as intermediaries either between rival groups of demonstrators or between demonstrators and the police. Monitoring groups were formed as a result of two distinct initiatives.

The Peace Accord had provided for the formation of the National Peace Secretariat and a number of Regional and Local Dispute Resolution Committees whose responsibilities included establishing rules and conditions related to marches and gatherings and liaising with police and magistrates on the same issues. Although the Dispute Resolution Committees were never as widespread as was initially envisioned, they were effective in some areas, notably the Johannesburg area, in establishing monitoring groups. Another approach was via the Network of Independent Monitors, which was set up in late 1992 and involved more than seventy organisations from across South Africa (Cawthra 1993:177).

The monitoring groups drew their active membership from a wide range of organisations within civil society, including human rights and legal support groups, peace groups and church-based groups, but they also involved activists from within both the ANC and IFP. They addressed a wide range of localised concerns including monitoring police investigations and complaints against the police, responding to and countering rumours, and threats and acts of violence. They were also involved in co-ordinating the international monitoring programme which ran from 1992 to 1994, initially to address the concerns of political violence and later to ensure that the electoral process was free and fair (COMSA 1993).

One of the key areas for monitors was in facilitating peaceful demonstrations and rallies. The monitoring groups trained volunteers who would attend public events and intercede between the police and local people in order to reduce the threat of clashes at demonstrations and act as crisis managers at a sign of violence breaking out. The monitors liased with the organisers of public gatherings and the police at both local and regional level in order to try to reach agreements over the nature of the planned events, the routes they should take and any specific local concerns that needed to be addressed.

On the day of public gatherings the monitors wore distinctive jackets or other markers. They would liaise with and to some extent co-ordinate the marshals on one side and the police commander on the other to ensure that both sides did their utmost to maintain the peace. On occasions monitors had to physically place themselves between rival political groups or between demonstrators and the police to prevent violence breaking out, but wherever possible urgent consultations sufficed. Besides crisis management, the monitors also took responsibility for ensuring that the necessary infrastructure of support was provided: first aid posts, water points and that police positions were clearly defined and routes were agreed.

At times monitors were physically threatened but in general they were treated with some respect. While many monitors came from outside the townships they also drew on local people when possible and utilised their authority and experience to influence events. Wherever possible the monitoring groups were mixed, they included members of both ANC and INF within each volunteer group. The ANC activists would act as lead monitors in ANC areas and Inkatha monitors did likewise in their areas, but it was important that the individuals were regarded principally as monitors rather than political activists.

Although they were initially treated with some suspicion both by political activists and by the police, all sides came to see the benefits of having monitors on the ground. The political groups saw that the monitors had some influence with the police and they could achieve things on the day by working through the monitors that they would not have been able to achieve in direct negotiation with the police. The police in turn were able to keep their officers away from the front line and devolve responsibility to the monitors and the marshals to ensure the events passed peacefully.

Independent monitoring at public gatherings was successful in many instances; for example, at a number of demonstrations around the time of the funeral of murdered ANC leader

Chris Hani in March 1993 (COMSA 1993). However some large demonstrations were still extremely problematic to control and in spite of the best efforts violence still occurred on occasions: in the run-up to the elections in 1994 a large Inkatha rally through Johannesburg degenerated into widespread violence as it past the ANC headquarters in the city and over fifty people were killed. In his report into the violence Judge Goldstone reiterated the need to provide an effective legal mechanism for the regulation of such events, such as those suggested in the recommendations made in the report that his commission had published the previous year.

The monitoring continued through the period of the elections when demonstrations were widespread and often tense and although some independent monitoring groups continue to function, they no longer operate on the scale of the early 1990s.

Reforming the Police

One of the key practical impacts that the system of independent monitoring had on the practical expression of the right to demonstrate was in reducing face to face confrontation between demonstrators and the police. The debate on the need for fundamental reform of the South African Police Force had been underway for some time. Much had been made of the localised systems of community policing that had been established under the apartheid regime and the possibility that these would provide models for future systems of criminal justice (Brogden and Shearing 1993; Cawthra 1993; Mayekiso 1996).

The monitoring system provided a more formalised experiment of such a new system. The fact that the police were willing to participate and withdraw from the front line on occasions indicated a degree of recognition for the need for reform. The success of the monitors demonstrated that in certain circumstances community policing could provide a viable alternative to lethal force in controlling potentially violent situation. Finally the willingness of the ANC and IFP to increase and improve the marshalling of their own supporters suggested that they were also focused on reducing violent confrontation as part of the normative political process.

Reform of the policing system has been one of the main achievements of the multi-party system. Although there are concerns as to its effectiveness (Shaw et al 1997), the development of community input into both on the ground policing practices and into structures of accountability has been a major change from the previous approach. One of the principal areas of reform has been with regard to the riot police, who were widely used in crowd control situations and often criticised for a too ready recourse to lethal force.

The former Internal Stability Division has been renamed as the Public Order Police and new organisational structures and systems of operation have begun to be implemented. All officers have undergone or will undergo a new training programme, while new crowd control tactics and techniques and methods of operational planning have been applied on the ground. Initial statistics from the 1996 Public Order Police Annual Report indicate that there has been a drop in the amount of unrest at crowd control incidents and a large decline in attacks on the police at such events. The report also indicates that while crowds were still dispersed by use of dogs, teargas, rubber bullets and water canon on a number of occasions, their use had declined over the previous two years. In contrast there had been an increase in the number of such situations that had been resolved by negotiation.

Although these reforms are at an early stage the initial indications suggest that changes are moving in the right direction (O'Rawe and Moore 1997). They also illustrate that it is possible to undertake a thorough and largely acceptable reform of an institution that had been completely identified with the previous political regime.

Legal Rights to Demonstrate

The new legislation dealing with the control of demonstrations was enacted in January 1994. However, it did not come into force until November 1996 and at the time of our research trip (September 1997) had been little used. At the same time the new South African Constitution also provided a guarantee of the right to demonstrate. Section 17 of the Bill of Rights chapter of the Constitution states simply that *'Everyone has the right, peacefully and unarmed, to assemble, to demonstrate, to picket and to present petitions'*. These rights are clarified and elaborated in the Regulation of Gatherings Act 1993 which is largely based on the recommendations contained in the Goldstone Commission report of 1992. The guiding principles of the act are set out in the preamble:

> Whereas every person has the right to assemble with other persons and to express his views on any matter freely in public and to enjoy the protection of the State while doing so;

> And whereas the exercise of such right shall take place peacefully and with due regards to the rights of others.

The peaceful exercise of the right to assembly is the joint responsibility of the convenor (organiser) of the event, an authorised member of the police and a responsible officer of the local authority. The responsible officer has the responsibility for co-ordinating the implementation of the procedures and also has the power to impose conditions and ban events, if he feels it is necessary for public order.

Notification and Conditions

The convenor of a gathering must give at least seven days notice to a responsible officer of the municipal authorities of any intended gathering. Notification should provide the names and addresses of the organisers, the purpose of the gathering, the time and place of assembly, the route to be taken and the time, place and means of dispersal and any details of transportation to and from the assembly and dispersal points.

The responsible officer must consult with the police over any problems concerning the proposed gathering. If the police raise any concerns then the responsible officer must call a meeting of the organisers, the police and any other relevant groups to try to reach agreement over any changes that are proposed. If no meeting is called within 24 hours, then the convenor can assume the gathering can take place as planned.

If no agreement is reached over changes to the plans then the responsible officer can impose conditions on the gathering. His main concerns are to ensure that vehicular or pedestrian traffic is not too severely disrupted, that access is available to property and workplaces, that rival gatherings are kept at an appropriate distance and to prevent any injury to persons or damage to property. Any conditions or restrictions that are imposed should be given in writing to the convenor of the gathering and to the police. The convenor has the responsibility of ensuring that every marshal knows the terms of the conditions that are imposed and the police should ensure that every officer is similarly aware. If there is a serious threat that the gathering will cause disruption to traffic, injury to persons or damage to property which the police could not contain, then the responsible officer can prohibit the gathering.

Appeals

If conditions are imposed without agreement or a gathering is prohibited, then the convenor has a right of appeal. Similarly if the responsible officer refuses a request by the police for conditions to be imposed or a gathering to be banned, then the police have the right to appeal.

In the first instance appeals should be made to an appropriate magistrate and must be lodged within 24 hours of any decision by the responsible officer. Furthermore, the convenor, the police and any other persons whose rights might be affected by the gathering can also oppose the magistrate's decision by appealing to the Supreme Court. The police have the responsibility of upholding the final decision of the courts, whether this might be to permit, to prohibit or to impose conditions on a gathering.

Conduct at Demonstrations

The law lays down a number on standard responsibilities and constraints on the organisers that are applicable to all public gatherings. The convenor is responsible for providing adequate marshals to ensure that the gathering is peaceful at all times. The marshals and other participants should also be aware of any terms or conditions imposed on the gathering and that the agreed route is followed. Marshals are also responsible for ensuring that free access is maintained to buildings and property during the gathering. General restrictions are also made on the wearing of mask, the carrying of dangerous weapons or the wearing uniforms that resemble those worn by the security forces. There is also a prohibition on speech, singing or signs that might incite hatred and on performing acts or uttering words that might cause or encourage violence.

Police Responsibilities

The police have a responsibility to ensure that all gatherings take place on the agreed route and under the agreed or imposed conditions, and that gatherings do not cause unnecessary disruption to traffic or the free movement of others. They also have responsibility for providing protection for any gathering, legal or otherwise, that takes place, and this includes preventing persons from interfering with or attempting to interfere with a gathering.

If the police have reasonable grounds to believe that danger to persons or property cannot be avoided then they can call on the people participating in the gathering to disperse. If necessary they can physically disperse the demonstrators. The force used should be proportionate to the circumstances and police should not use weapons likely to cause serious bodily injury or death. However, if there is a serious threat to life or attempt to injure people or cause damage to property, then the police are permitted to use firearms and other weapons.

Responsibilities and Penalties

If damage occurs as a result of a gathering or demonstration then depending on the circumstances, the convenors, the organisations involved or each individual participating can be held responsible and liable.

Any person who convenes an illegal gathering, fails to comply with constraints, ignores the general restraints or hinders, obstructs or resists a police officer, a responsible officer, a convenor or a marshal at a gathering can be liable to a fine of up to R20 000 (£3,000) and imprisonment for up to one year.

Successful Reforms?

The Regulation of Gatherings Act attempts to provide a comprehensive system and structure to regulate and facilitate demonstrations and marches. Much of the law is familiar from reviews of legislation in other countries, but perhaps the most interesting facet is the recognition of the inherent political nature of such public gatherings. This is acknowledged through the interlocking structure of the decision making process which links the organisers, the police and the civil authorities as mutually responsible participants in the democratic process. In so doing it demands that each party recognise their role in maintaining the balance between human rights and social responsibilities.

Laws often look fair and balanced in their drafting and it is often only through their practical implementation that the cracks in their logic and loopholes begin to appear. In recognising the political nature of the regulatory process, the law also acknowledges the potential for abuse and bias in the ability to exercise one's rights. It is therefore probably a vital factor that there is the opportunity to appeal through the courts against any arbitrarily imposed decision on whether a gathering should take place or not.

As with so many politically contentious issues it is possible to devise a system and structure that looks good on paper, but the key question is whether the participants in the process are willing to work with it or whether they prefer to work against it. So far the Regulation of Gatherings Act has not been widely challenged and the police have not had to face the same degree of violent confrontation. Since the 1994 election, demonstrations and gatherings have not been particularly contentious or violent and although some gatherings, notably those organised by a radical Muslim group PAGAD (People Against Gangsterism and Drugs) have been banned under the new law, to date these prohibitions have not been challenged. It seems likely that this situation will remain until the run-up to the next elections in 1999 when once again demonstrations will increase in number and contention. With luck by then the political organisations will have become used to operating within the new legal structure and the reforms that have been initiated with the police service will have matured sufficiently for the new practices to have become the norm.

PART THREE

General Principles

The case studies illustrate a number of ways of addressing the ways and means by which freedom of assembly and the right to demonstrate are facilitated in practice in a diverse range of countries. While no single example provides a clear analogy or mirror to the situation in Northern Ireland, collectively they can be used to highlight a number of factors relevant to the current disputes here.

At the most general level we are interested in the relationship between law and practice, between legal and constitutional guarantees for civil rights and how these are played out on the streets. Constitutional rights and legal frameworks often relate to idealised situations rather than the messy and varied issues that arise from daily life.

On issues of public order there is always a balance to be maintained between law enforcement and keeping the peace. Sometimes the letter of the law must be allowed to be broken in order to maintain a wider peace. Sometimes the law must be changed if the situation that the law applies to changes.

There are a number of limited issues that recur when dealing with the practice of demonstrating. There is a narrow repertoire of problems that need to be addressed and despite the varieties of local context there is also a narrow range of practical solutions that can be imposed whilst still working within a human rights framework.

In the section that follows we draw out some of these practical solutions which appear to be of most relevance to Northern Ireland. Not all of them may be of use here and no single country could provide a ready-made model of a workable solution to the current disputes. We do not hold up these practices as necessarily providing all the answers to the disputes over the right to parade here. Rather we use them to illustrate that there are a variety of ways forward and we suggest that they represent current international best practice with respect to the basic right of freedom of assembly.

Each of the countries we have surveyed has faced some degree of difficulty over public demonstrations and each has addressed the problem to a greater or lesser extent. The variety of approaches illustrates that every problem has more than one solution.

1. Constitutional Guarantees

In Northern Ireland there is no constitutional guarantee of freedom of assembly or of rights to public political expression. Rights exist only as common law in so far as that which is not prohibited or restricted is permitted. It has been suggested that any constitutional settlement in Northern Ireland should include a Bill of Rights. This argument has received widespread support from across the political spectrum.

- A number of countries, including Canada, Ireland, Italy, South Africa and the USA, have a constitutional guarantee of freedom of assembly.

- In most of these, this freedom is qualified, by extending that right to peaceful assembly or to assembly without arms.

- Furthermore, freedom of assembly is but one of a number of such constitutional freedoms, which are of a similar or equal status. Freedom of assembly is thus always limited and balanced by other constitutional freedoms.

- As a constitutional right, freedom of assembly applies equally to all members of and all sections of society. It is not conditional, nor subject to approval of either the majority community or minorities within the society.

- Constitutional rights are, or can be, limited by concerns for public order, public safety, public health (Italy) and morality (Ireland, Italy) and 'other reasonable limits' (Canada).

- Such unspecified or unfocused restrictions may be or can be clarified by the courts. In Italy and the USA the courts have overturned laws which they consider unduly restrict constitutional guarantees. In Canada and South Africa the constitutional limits have yet to be addressed by the judiciary.

- Three of the countries (France, Israel and the United Kingdom) that we studied provided no constitutional right to demonstrate, although in each country such rights had been established through practice.

2. Legal Frameworks

All countries have a range of laws that are used to govern the practical limits of the freedom of assembly and rights to demonstrate. In Northern Ireland the right to parade has been managed under the 1987 Public Order (NI) Order. Much of this legislation will be replaced by the new Public Processions (NI) Act (see Appendix for a summary of the main provisions).

- In France and the United Kingdom the right to demonstrate is guaranteed neither by constitution nor legal framework, but rather through the absence of formal restrictions. Under English common law one is allowed to do something unless it is prohibited.

- Israel has a somewhat intermediate position is so far as there is no constitutional right to freedom of assembly. However, the Supreme Court has defined it as a 'fundamental right'. As such the government has issued legally binding directives to define the framework of such rights.

- In France, Ireland, Italy and the United Kingdom laws defining or limiting the rights of assembly were introduced during periods of political disturbances during the 1930s, when there were widespread and recurrent clashes between political opponents of the left and right. In each country these regulations still provide the basis for legal constraint.

- In South Africa a new legal framework defining the structure of management of demonstrations was introduced as a result of a commission of inquiry into public violence following serious violence at political demonstrations during the period of political transition.

- In each country laws have been enacted to define or to limit the constitutional rights with respect to concerns for public disorder. In all cases public order is cited as a legitimate reason for banning or restricting a public demonstration.

- Constraints can also be legally imposed for reasons such as support for unconstitutional demands (France has banned demonstrations in support of the legalisation of cannabis) or support for illegal organisations (Ireland).

3. Tradition

In Northern Ireland many parades that have been held for a number of years are considered to be 'traditional'. Some believe that 'traditional' parades have greater rights than other non-traditional parades. At various times in the past the significance of traditional parades has been singled out in law. Under the Public Processions Act the Parades Commission will have to take into consideration 'the desirability of allowing a procession customarily held along a particular route to be held along that route' as one factor when making determinations over contentious parades.

- The concept of traditional rights was not acknowledged as a legal category in any of the other countries that we studied. However some informal recognition was given to longstanding parading practices.

- Traditional rights to demonstrate, at particular times of the year or over specific routes, are rarely invoked elsewhere. In most cases a pragmatic and flexible approach is adopted. Routes are varied according to circumstances and change over the years.

- In Canada and USA there is a comparable concept of grandfathering under which long established or important events have a right to either a specific route or a specific date or both.

- In New York and Toronto there are a limited number of grandfathered parades each year, although the number can increase and has done so in recent years. Many parades are organised by distinct ethnic communities; in neither city does any single community have more than one grandfathered parade a year.

- The New York St Patrick's Day parade is the longest established parade. Under the grandfathering system only the Ancient Order of Hibernians are permitted to organise a parade on Fifth Avenue on 17 March. Nevertheless the route has changed on a number of occasions.

- Grandfathering does not necessarily imply a longstanding practice, the Khalsa parade, organised by the Sikh community and the West Indian Caribana carnival parade in Toronto are both of recent origin, but both are now considered to have the same rights as long established grandfathered events.

- In London and Paris there are established or favoured routes for large demonstrations, but these are not claimed by particular groups, nor are there specific rights to use them. In Paris there are also favoured areas for left-wing demonstrations and others for right-wing demonstrations, but again these traditions are very flexible.

- Tradition therefore exists as a limited concept in some other countries, but it does not transcend other concerns for public order or disruption to daily routines.

4. Equal Rights

It is widely acknowledged the human and civil rights should be applied equally and without discrimination to all members and sections of society. In many countries equal rights have been acknowledged in law but denied in practice. In Northern Ireland the right to demonstrate has not been extended equally to all people and all communities. Nationalists have argued that their rights to demonstrate have often been denied while Unionists feel that their rights are currently under threat. Recognition of mutual rights is an important feature of any democratic civil society.

- Whether it is guaranteed by the constitution or by the law it is widely accepted that the right to demonstrate should be given or permitted to all members of a society equally.

- Nevertheless in some countries specific communities or political groups may feel that they are discriminated against over the right to hold demonstrations. In a number of countries the gay community have had to fight for their right to demonstrate in recent years, although their Gay Pride parades have become established events in many cities.

- In Israel, despite an active assertion of a general right to demonstrate as a fundamental right, this right is not applied equally to both Jewish and Arab citizens of the state. Arab Israelis believe that their civil rights to political expression and commemoration are not upheld with equal force to those of Jewish Israelis. However, it is felt that the situation is improving through more assertive actions.

- In France and the United Kingdom the political parties of the extreme right feel that their rights to demonstrate are not safeguarded by the state in the same way as the rights of other political parties. In Italy similar feelings have been expressed by federalist parties.

- There is also clearly an issue when tradition is invoked to give one particular community rights to demonstrate that are not offered to other communities. In many cases this is overcome by giving each community access to traditional events.

- Where rights are not extended to all sections of the community equally there is clearly an issue for the state or for the courts to address. Similarly when one political group or community seeks to prevent another one from exercising its civil rights the issue should be dealt with promptly rather than be quietly ignored.

5. Notification

Under the new Public Processions Act organisers of parades and demonstrations will have to give 28 days notice of their intention to hold a public procession. Organisers of protest meetings will have to give 14 days notice of their intentions. Notification is given to the police on a standard form who then forward the information to the Parades Commission.

- In all countries surveyed, except the Republic of Ireland, there is a requirement to notify an authority of plans to organise a demonstration, parade or march. In all countries surveyed exceptions are allowed when it is not possible to give even the minimum notification period.

- In Canada, England, France, Israel, Italy and the USA notification must be given to the local police. In Scotland and South Africa notification is given to the elected municipal authorities that have the responsibility of liaising with the police.

- The required period of notification varies from three days in Italy to twenty-one days in Canada. In practice even the three days notification period is not strictly adhered to in Italy while in Canada the police prefer to be given even longer notice wherever possible. In England and Scotland, local agreements mean that the loyal orders usually give much longer notice of their intentions.

- In most jurisdictions notification is notice of intent, rather than a request for permission to demonstrate, although in Israel organisers must receive formal permission. The authorities require information on the time, place and scale of the demonstration. They also want to know the reason for the event and the name and address of those taking responsibility for its organisation.

- Notification usually leads to a process of negotiation over the time and route that is proposed for the demonstration. There is no generally accepted right that one can demonstrate wherever and whenever one wants. Some form of compromise is normally reached between the organisers and the authorities.

- In France, Israel and Italy any decision to prohibit or restrict a demonstration should be notified in advance of the event. In France and Italy this is to allow time for negotiations, in Israel it is to allow for an appeal to the courts.

- In France the police and the organisers sign formal documents that indicate the agreed terms of the event. This imposes a responsibility on the organisers to follow the agreed route, time etc and on the police to protect a legal demonstration.

- If no prior notification is given of a demonstration then the event is deemed illegal. In all countries surveyed the police have the right to disperse such gathering while the organisers of illegal demonstrations can be subject to prosecution. In practice the police often facilitate illegal demonstrations in the interests of public order.

6. Constraints

At present the RUC have the power to impose a variety of constraints on the organisers of demonstrations relating to the route, the timing and the content of the procession, but only if they have concerns for public order. Under the new legislation the Parades Commission will take over such powers and have produced a Code of Conduct which sets out a broad range of standards that should be adhered to. The Parades Commission will also be expected to consider the impact a parade will have on relationships within the community and any disruption likely to be caused to the life of a community before imposing constraints. The RUC will retain the right to impose constraints due to fears for public order on the day of a parade. Only the Secretary of State can ban one or more parades in their entirety.

- In all countries the authorities responsible for the policing of parades have the power to ban parades or impose conditions on them. The total prohibition of a parade is rarely exercised, in most cases the authorities would expect to reach some form of negotiated compromise if there were any problems with the proposed event.

- The most common reason for constraining or banning public demonstrations is concern for public order. However public order is a poorly defined concept. It is generally accepted that public order means an absence of violence, but it is not clear how far it also refers either to an absence of disruption of daily life or to what constitutes the norm of public order.

- Usually the police have considerable flexibility to determine the limits of public order and make a judgement on what might constitute a threat to it. However, in Israel the police are required to have more concrete evidence of active planning for violence before they can ban an event as a threat to public order.

- Often the threat of a counter-demonstration or of some form of protest is sufficient to invoke concerns for public order and prohibit the original event. But in Italy the courts have decided that in such a situation the original demonstration should be permitted and the counter-event should be banned or constrained.

- In France demonstrations can be banned by the police if they support or advocate illegal activities. This power is rarely exercised although a proposed pro-cannabis demonstration was banned recently. In contrast demonstrations against visiting heads of state or important foreign visitors are often banned, heavily constrained or subject to intensive security.

- In Italy demonstrations can be banned by the questore if there are concerns for public health or morality, similarly in Ireland demonstrations can be restricted on the grounds of concern for morality. There is no indication that these concerns have ever been invoked.

- In most cases the authorities are also concerned about disruption that may be caused to daily routines. In Canada, France and the USA there is a concern to minimise the disruption to traffic and free movement of other users of urban areas. In Canada and the USA the disruption to commercial life and business is also a key factor in the timing or location of a demonstration.

- In contrast, in Israel the courts have determined that demonstrations are an important feature of democratic life and therefore demonstrators have as much right to use the streets as pedestrians and vehicles.

- In a number of countries demonstrations are, or can be, banned from sensitive locations. Parliament buildings, government buildings and courts frequently have restricted access. In New York demonstrations are also banned from passing the United Nations building.

- In Israel demonstrations are usually banned if they are likely to provoke religious hostility. Jewish demonstrations have been banned from some strongly Palestinian areas, and Jews are not allowed onto the Temple Mount in Jerusalem. Palestinian demonstrations are generally restricted within Israel.

7. Time, Place and Manner

Under the new legislation and the Code of Conduct the Parades Commission will be able to impose constraints on the route of a parade, on the time of a parade and on the style and content of a parade. Any such restrictions should only be imposed if mutual agreement has not been reached as a result of local dialogue or more formal negotiations.

- In the USA any restrictions imposed on the right to demonstrate are readily challenged through the courts. Nevertheless the police are able to invoke their right to restrict the time, place and manner of a demonstration without limiting basic civil rights. It is accepted that while people have the right to demonstrate this will not always be facilitated in the time, place or manner of their own choosing.

- While this is not explicitly formulated elsewhere, in most, if not all, jurisdictions the authorities reserve the right to limit the time, place and manner of a demonstration.

- Sometimes time, place and manner restrictions are imposed because of concerns for public order or in order to avoid too much disruption to daily life. Sometimes changes are imposed to avoid undue restrictions on the civil rights of others. Sometimes restrictions are imposed for the convenience of the police or other authorities.

- In New York the police have imposed an arbitrary limit on the number of parades that they will permit on Fifth Avenue each year. As the main thoroughfare it is a popular route, but demonstrations along it disrupt city life and make undue demands on the police.

- Similarly in Boston the police prefer to restrict the number of outdoor public events that are held on any one day. Restrictions are also imposed on the number of events held on weekdays or in areas where they will cause too much disruption. New events are therefore likely to be assigned the downtown commercial area on a Sunday in winter.

- In Toronto the police will restrict the route of any demonstration if it is likely to disrupt trade and they favour Sundays for public assemblies.

- In London large demonstrations in the West End are encouraged to use 'traditional' and easily policed routes and are not readily allowed on weekdays because of the disruption they can cause to traffic.

- In each of these cases the right to demonstrate is upheld, but the context of the demonstration is largely determined by the authorities rather than by the organisers. Where possible this is done as a result of discussions or negotiations, rather than by arbitrary imposition.

8. Opposition

Attempting to stop a legal demonstration is an offence under the Public Order (NI) Order and will remain so under the new Public Processions (NI) Act. However the RUC have often responded to crowds of protesters by restraining a hitherto legal parade on the grounds that to do otherwise would cause serious disruption to public order. Unionists have complained that the police have failed to enforce the law, nationalists have insisted on their right to prevent parades going where they are not wanted. The result has been to undermine faith in the rule of law.

- All public demonstrations make statements about the issues a group supports or opposes and demonstrations are, or should be able to be, provocative. They are therefore likely to provoke opposition or reaction from outsiders.

- While it is widely accepted that demonstrations should be allowed to be provocative, all countries agree that there are limits to acceptable provocation; demonstrations should not be allowed to provoke fear or encourage violence. In many countries sensitivity is also paid to local ethnic or racial differences when considering the likely provocation a demonstration might cause.

- Although many demonstrations may well provoke hostile opposition, it is generally accepted that such opposition should not be permitted to stop a legal demonstration.

- In the USA the police accept that a 'hostile audience' should be allowed to protest within 'sight and sound' of the target of their hostility, but should not be allowed to prevent the other demonstration from taking place.

- In Israel the police are expected to protect legal demonstrations from hostile audiences even if the demonstration is being deliberately offensive. Police have protected demonstrators who mocked or satirised religious symbols.

- In France and Italy counter-demonstrations are usually permitted relatively near to the demonstration that they are opposing, but are not allowed to interfere with it. In France the police have a responsibility to protect the right of legal demonstrations to follow their agreed route.

- However, in spite of these assertions of upholding the right of legal demonstrations in practice counter-demonstrators are sometimes able to stop them or force them to be re-routed. It is not unusual for far right or neo-Nazi demonstrations to be confronted and stopped in France, the UK and the USA by left-wing opponents.

9. Provocation and Fear

The public order legislation in Northern Ireland makes it an offence to incite fear, provocation and hatred towards people of different religious beliefs, colour, race, nationality, citizenship and ethnic and national origins, by the use of words or behaviour or through the display of written material in a public place.

- It is widely accepted that demonstrations can be restricted, re-routed or banned if there is concern that there is a deliberate attempt to provoke violence, to provoke fear or if there is a reasonable fear of a violent reaction.

- In all countries town or city centres are usually regarded as neutral zones and all sections of the community have a right to demonstrate in such areas. Provocative demonstrations would usually be tolerated in such areas.

- There are exceptions however. In France provocative demonstrations against a foreign state are often prohibited or restricted, many of these are planned for the centre of Paris. In Italy demonstrations that are considered seditious or against the state can be banned.

- Residential neighbourhoods are more sensitive areas for demonstrations and there would be more concern about the nature of any such public assemblies.

- Although the US Supreme Court eventually ruled that a neo-Nazi group should have been allowed to demonstrate in the heart of Skokie, a largely Jewish suburb of Chicago, other countries would be less tolerant of such behaviour.

- In South Africa the police were wary of any ANC demonstrations that aimed to go near to Inkhata areas or vice versa.

- In Israel Jewish demonstrations are not usually allowed to pass through specifically Palestinian areas and, in general, caution is given to the sanctioning of demonstrations by outsiders in strongly Orthodox areas.

10. Appealing Constraints

At present there is no right of appeal against restrictions imposed on parades by the RUC. Under the Public Processions Act only the Chief Constable will have the right to appeal a determination of the Parades Commission. Although there is a general right to seek a judicial review of decisions concerning parades the judiciary will only consider whether the correct procedure has been followed and will not review the decision itself.

- All countries accept that an agent of state authority will have power to ban or to impose constraints on a demonstration. Constraints or changes to original plans are usually arrived at through negotiation with the organisers, however an agreed compromise is not always possible. In most countries some means of appeal against restrictions is possible.

- In Israel the Supreme Court has been willing to hear an appeal against police restrictions on a demonstration at very short notice. On a number of occasions bans or restrictions have been overturned. The court actions have also led to clear directives being set out by the government to define the rights and limits that should structure police decision making.

- In South Africa the newly enacted Regulation of Gatherings Act allows for the possibility of appeal against restrictions on demonstrations. This has not been taken up to date.

- In France, Italy and the USA appeals must go through the normal court system and therefore can take a considerable time. In the USA the Supreme Court has regularly overturned legal and bureaucratic constraints on the right to demonstrate, but cases often take several years to go through the complete judicial process.

- In each case, until the appeal process has been completed, the original constraints on the demonstration remain in force.

- An appeal may well consolidate, establish or extend the right of demonstrators but because of the long time-scale involved may have little impact on their ability to hold the demonstration in the manner desired.

11. Policing

The RUC have overall and final responsibility for public order. The RUC will be expected to advise the Parades Commission of their assessment of the public order implications of any parade. The Chief Constable, alone, has the right to appeal to the Secretary of State against a determination of the Parades Commission. The RUC also have the right to invoke concerns for public order on the day of a parade and so overturn otherwise legally binding determinations.

- In all jurisdictions the police are responsible both for maintaining public order and for facilitating the right of public assembly. They also have a duty to minimise disruption caused by demonstrations.

- Policing demonstrations often also involves balancing concerns for law enforcement with those of public order. As a result illegal demonstrations sometimes have to be facilitated in order to minimise the risk of more serious disorder.

- In an ideal situation the involvement of police at demonstrations should be kept to a minimum level. In many cases the police do little more than control the traffic and maintain a discrete visible presence.

- Ideal policing also involves working in conjunction with the organisers of a demonstration. Good lines of communication are an essential factor. In New York officers from the community relations department act as intermediaries between demonstrators and the front line police. In France the organisers of a demonstration are expected to be at its head where they can be easily contacted.

- In New York the police also have lawyers present to ensure that their officers comply with the letter of the law and that the rights of demonstrators are not ignored.

- Given their responsibilities for public order, the police must always be ready to deal with potential trouble. In all countries there are either special riot police units or specific riot training is given to all officers. Usually riot police are kept in reserve, at a distance or out of sight until or unless they are required.

- A limited repertoire of weapons is used for riot control. The standard equipment includes helmets, shields and batons. Tear gas and water cannons are also available in a number of countries.

- At times live ammunition is, or has been, used against demonstrators or protesters. In Israel live ammunition is used against Palestinian demonstrators, but never against Jewish Israelis. In South Africa live ammunition was used under the apartheid regime, and was available in Italy until the early 1980s.

- Only the Israeli security forces use rubber or plastic bullets. They have never been considered as an option in Italy. In France they were tried, but were considered too dangerous.

- In situations of serious political or social conflict the police are often regarded as partial and are identified by demonstrators as an opponent. Police action or even their presence at demonstrations can therefore provoke rather than restrain rioting and other violence.

- Violent clashes between demonstrators and police occurred frequently in Italy in the late 1940s and early 1950s and again during the 1970s; in South Africa in the late 1980s and early 1990s and clashes continue between the Israeli security forces and Palestinians.

- In Italy the reform and demilitarisation of the police in 1981 was a factor in reducing the political violence. Similarly in South Africa reform and restructuring of the police force has been an essential part of the transition from apartheid to democracy.

12. Civil Control - Stewards and Monitors

The organisers of parades and protests always taken some responsibility for the stewarding of their events. However, this has not always been as effective as it might have been. Under the draft Code of Conduct, issued by the Parades Commission, stewarding assumes greater importance and there is emphasis on the use of individuals who have been trained to understand their duties and responsibilities. While the police will retain ultimate responsibility for crowd control, stewards can be expected to be involved in crowd management and ensuring that the any conditions that have been imposed are made known to all participants.

- The police are responsible for public order, but much of the responsibility for the practical policing of demonstrations falls on the organisers. In all countries the organisers of parades are expected to provide adequate stewards. This is never usually set out in any formal manner and the number of stewards that are needed will largely depend on the scale of the event.

- Stewards are expected to be both identified and identifiable. Usually this involves little more than a coloured armband or top. In some situations stewards will be expected to have walkie-talkies or other forms of mobile communication.

- Stewards rarely receive any formal training except through a culminative process of attending demonstrations. They should be aware of their responsibilities and of any agreements over the route, style or form of the demonstration.

- Stewards are usually responsible for controlling order within the body of demonstrators and any reactions to protesters. They are not responsible for the behaviour of people outside the body of the demonstration.

- In Italy the organisers and the stewards are responsible for all individuals and groups that turn up to participate in a demonstration. However, in France the organisers can define the limits to the body of the demonstration and insist that police take responsibility for specific groups who often join in at the end with the aim of causing trouble.

- In South Africa a system of independent monitors was established at a time when there was increasing violence at political demonstrations. The monitors were volunteers and drawn from activists in the voluntary sector, the churches and other sectors of civil society.

- Under the apartheid regime the South African Police Force was widely regarded as a partial body that too often resorted to lethal force to control public order. The monitors acted as intermediaries between the police and rival ANC and Inkhata groups.

- The monitors were a neutral and unarmed 'policing' body who sought to defuse tensions and control disturbances at demonstrations. Monitors liaised with both the organisers of demonstrations and with the police. They were used to ensure that the official police were less frequently involved in dealing with minor disturbances that could often quickly spiral into more serious trouble as demonstrators reacted to the police.

- The monitoring system lasted for several years through the period of transition and groups were set up in a number of areas where political tensions were high. Their interventions were often regarded as highly successful in maintaining order while enabling demonstrations to take place. Most groups were disbanded after the elections in 1994.

- In New York the NYPD Community Relations Division acts in a similar manner to mediate between the officers policing the demonstration and the organisers of public events. While they are serving officers, they have no operational responsibilities at the demonstration. They are distinguished by wearing a different uniform from the operational officers. They work from the office of the Chief of Police and have direct communication to senior level if they feel that the policing is being handled badly.

13. Alcohol

Consumption of alcohol has been acknowledged as one source of problems at parades and it is widely accepted that this issue needs to be dealt with. To date the RUC appear to have been reluctant to address this problem. Under the new legislation the police will have greater powers to confiscate alcohol being carried or consumed in the vicinity of a parade route and to stop and search vehicles going to parades if it is suspected that they are carrying alcohol. It remains to be seen whether such powers will be exercised.

- The consumption of alcohol is a prominent feature of many public celebrations. Some degree of licence is given to public drinking at demonstrations on public holidays and carnival or carnival-like events. However, there is always a fragile balance between acceptable use and over-consumption and abuse.

- In both Boston and New York excessive public drinking on St Patrick's Day had become a serious problem by the 1980s. Drunkenness led to extensive violence and attacks on police officers.

- In the late 1980s new regimes were introduced to prohibit on street drinking and police were empowered to confiscate alcohol in the vicinity of the parades. The police feel that within a few years the nature of the parades had changed and had become more family orientated and publicly acceptable events.

- In Toronto similar problems were associated with the West Indian Caribana parade and festival. While less severe restrictions were imposed, the police were able to constrain the sale and consumption of alcohol to specific areas of the celebrations.

- There is also an issue of the consumption of illegal drugs at some events like the Toronto Carabana festival and the Notting Hill Carnival. In both cities police have said that they are conscious of the potential for charges of racial harassment in such situations and accept that some degree of licence must be given.

Appendices

Commentary: The Public Processions (N.I.) Bill

Clause 1 & 2 - The Parades Commission and it's Duties.
The Bill sets out the duties of the Commission:
- to promote understanding on issues concerning parades;
- to mediate and promote mediation;
- to issue determinations on particular public processions;
- to monitor the conduct of public processions;
- to keep under review the operation of the act.

Clauses 3, 4 & 5 - Procedures, Guidelines and Codes of Conduct.
The Commission is required to produce a Code of Conduct giving guidance to those in processions, Procedural Rules by which the practices of the Commission will be regulated, and a set of Guidelines, under which determinations made by the Commission will be made.

Clause 6 - Notification of a Procession.
Requires that advance notification of a procession be given 28 days before the event, although there is provision to give shorter notice if there was good reason for not giving 28 days. Funeral processions or other processions of a class that might be specified by the Secretary of State are excluded. If a procession takes place without due notice being given, or differing in important respects from the information given in the notice, then an offence has been committed (up to 6 months in jail), unless the accused can prove that he did not knowingly fail to comply, or that the circumstances were beyond his control, or that he was complying with instructions from a member of the RUC not below the rank of inspector.

Clause 7 - Determinations
The Commission may issue a determination on the conditions under which a parade may take place under the Guidelines which shall take into account:
- the possibility of public disorder and likely damage to property;
- disruption to the life of the community ;
- impact on relationships within the community
- failure of organisers to comply with the Code of Conduct (presently or previously);
- the desirability of holding a procession customarily held along a particular route.

A person guilty of not complying with conditions imposed can be jailed for up to 2 years unless he can prove circumstances beyond his control or that he was acting under direction from a member of the RUC not below the rank of Inspector.

Clause 8 - The Chief Constable's leave to Appeal
Allows for the Chief Constable to make an appeal to the Secretary of State to review a determination made by the Commission. She may revoke, amend or confirm the determination having consulted the Commission's Guidelines and will notify the Commission who can no longer issue a determination on that specific procession.

Clause 9 - Powers of the RUC on the day.
Confirms the RUC's powers under common law to take action to deal with a breach of the peace. This effectively gives the RUC powers to deal with a public order situation on the day, regardless of a determination made by the Commission.

Clause 10 - Powers of the Secretary of State
The Secretary of State retains powers to prohibit a particular procession, type of procession or all processions in particular area taking into account:
- the possibility of public disorder and likely damage to property;
- disruption to the life of the community;
- impact on relationships within the community;
- the demands made on the police and military.

If possible the Secretary of State is to consult the Commission, the Chief Constable and Police Authority and any decision made revokes previous determinations made by the Commission.

Clause 11 - Registration of Bands
Provisions remains on the legislation for the registration of bands.

Clause 12 - Control of Alcohol
This gives the RUC specific powers over the control of alcohol at public processions. Alcohol can be confiscated from those in the vicinity of an event and also from a passenger vehicle carrying passengers to a place in the vicinity of a procession.

Clause 13 - Protesters
Any protester that attempts to prevent or hinder a lawful procession by
- hindering, molesting or obstructing a procession;
- acting in disorderly way towards a procession;
- behaving offensively and abusively towards participants in a procession;
- can be a guilty of an offence receiving up to 6 months imprisonment.

Other Points to Note:
- There is provision for the number of Commissioners including the chairman to be raised from five to seven.
- The quorum for a Commission meeting is three with the Chairman having a casting vote if necessary.
- Staff for the Commission are provided by the civil service of Northern Ireland or of the United Kingdom.
- The Commission will produce an annual report.

Commentary: The Parades Commission Procedural Rules

These set out the steps that the Parades Commission will take in making determinations about disputes. It assumes that some disputes will continue in areas where parades have been contentious over the past three years. The Commission will begin work in addressing these areas as soon as is practical and will not wait for the 28 days notification.

The work of the Commission is set out in a number of stages:

1. Gathering Information
Background information will be gathered by Authorised Officers (employees or field workers) who will aim to build relationships with local groups and interested parties. The information will include the details of past parades, the demographic mix of local communities and key points on the route of possible parades.

2. Taking Evidence
Members of the Commission will then take evidence, both written and oral, from as wide a range of local people as are willing to offer it. All evidence, both written and oral will be treated as confidential. The Commission can also seek out the opinion of specific individuals, groups or organisations.

3. Preliminary View
Having gathered information and taken evidence the Commission will offer a preliminary view of all contested parade locations. This will indicate whether any and what type of conditions might be imposed on any or all of the parades in a location. This preliminary view will not be legally binding.

4. Making Formal Determinations
If disputes persist despite local discussions and in the face of the preliminary view, then the Commission will review the situation. It may take fresh evidence up to 10 working days prior to the parade as well as taking advice from the RUC, before issuing a legally binding determination. Where possible determinations will be issued five working days in advance of a parade. Interested parties will be notified of the determination in writing.

5. Review of Determinations
In exceptional circumstances the Commission will consider fresh evidence and may reverse or revoke its initial determination.

Commentary: The Parades Commission Guidelines

The Guidelines provide the framework with which the Parades Commission (PC) will balance the conflicting rights of parade participants and the wider community.

- They emphasise that the right to peaceful assembly and freedom of expression are important, but not unlimited, rights.
- The exercise of these rights brings with it responsibilities to the wider community.
- These include a responsibility to seek resolution to disputes by peaceful means and a responsibility to abide by the law.
- Such responsibilities apply to those parading and to those protesting.

In making determinations the Commission must address five principal factors:

1. The threat of public disorder
The Commission will rely on the advice of the RUC and then consider public order alongside other factors.

2. Disruption to the life of the community.
All public events cause some disruption, so the Commission will have to balance the significance of the parade and the disruption that will be caused. Disruption should not necessarily stop the exercise of the right to parade. The Commission will judge whether the disruption caused is disproportionate to the significance of the procession to those participating. The Commission will consider: the duration of the procession and the degree of restriction placed on local residents, on businesses, on public amenities and on places of worship. In general, commercial areas will be regarded as neutral zones and the rights of parade participants will be upheld.

3. Impact on relationships within the community.
This will involve consideration of the nature of the route; the possibility of alternative routes; the local demographic balance; local sensitive sites; and the purpose of the parade. The Parades Commission will also consider the frequency and size of parades in a given area over the year and attempt to judge whether the parade is likely to create a sense of fear or intimidation for residents. It will judge the purpose of the parade; numbers taking part; past conduct of the parade; the regalia carried; the nature and number of bands. The Parades Commission will consider how far concerns of other members of the community have been addressed by parade organisers. The Commission will also consider the wider implications for Northern Ireland of any parade, both in the past and in the future.

4.Compliance with the Code of Conduct
The Commission will consider how far the parade organisers have been willing to comply with the Code of Conduct and how successful this had been on previous parades.

5.Tradition
The Commission recognises the importance given to long-standing parades and will weigh this along with other factors.

Commentary: The Parades Commission Code of Conduct

This document emphasises the responsibilities that parade organisers have towards the wider community. Much of it will be regarded as standard practice for the loyal orders.

Preparation
The emphasis in this section is on the responsibility that parade organisers have (a) to provide information to, and (b) to address the concerns of people living and working on the route of a parade. In general it recommends providing advance information to allow people to make arrangements for any potential disruption the parade might cause. It recommends that organisers should:

- notify local businesses of times of parades.
- liaise with local places of worship.
- notify residents on the route of planned parades (by notices in the local papers or using fly sheets) and attempt to address concerns of residents particularly those of 'another cultural identity'. A contact person should be identified for the purposes of liaison.
- liaise with police and provide adequate stewards capable of dealing with emergency situations.

2. Timing
It is essential that during the hours of darkness parades should begin and end at the times specified on the 11/1 form.

3. Bands
It is the responsibility of the parade organisers to ensure that all bands adhere to the terms of their contract and are aware of any conditions that have been imposed on the parade.

4. Stewards
An appropriate number of trained stewards should be provided. The number required will be determined by the scale of the parade. Stewards should be identified and identifiable.

5. Providing Notice
The new law requires that at least 28 days notice is given of parades. But the Commission sees no reason why longer notice should not be given to help general planning for events.

6. The Parade
On the parade itself the Commission again emphasises the need for well briefed stewards who are aware of any conditions or restrictions. Participants should also be aware of arrangements for a 'peaceful and rapid dispersal'.

7. Protest Meetings

Organisers wishing to hold a protest meeting are required, where practical, to give 14 days notice.

General Behaviour at Parades and Protests

Appendix A relates to general standards of behaviour on parades - emphasis is on responsibility to the rest of the community. It largely confirms existing parading practice.

Sections B. Dress, F. Music and G. Flags etc. all relate to the prohibition of displays of emblems, regalia and other symbols related to proscribed organisations.

Section H. Stewarding - reinforces the responsibility to provide trained, recognisable and responsible stewards.

Section K. organisers are responsible for ensuring that participants are aware of conditions imposed on parades.

Appendix B - Refers to areas of greater sensitivity and requirements of more respectful behaviour at places of worship, war memorials and cemeteries, interface areas and in areas of 'other cultural identities'. The emphasis is on the need for dignified and respectful behaviour.

Appendix C - Relates to standards of behaviour during protests against parades.

Section A. emphasises having due regard for the rights of others, avoiding the use of words and behaviours which could be perceived as provocative, threatening or abusive.

Sections B. and D. refer to the proscription of paramilitary uniforms or the displaying of flags of proscribed organistaions.

Section C. Location, demands that protesters should not obstruct a legal parade or the free flow of traffic.

Section D. Alcohol, suggests that an organiser of a protest should take necessary measures to remove a participant under the influence of alcohol.

Section F. Stewarding, reinforces the responsibility to provide trained, recognisable and responsible stewards.

Section G. H. and I.point out that organisers should ensure that all participants are informed of any conditions imposed by the police, ensure co-operation with the police, and disperse the protest quickly at the end.

Alleyne-Dettmers, P.T. (1996). *Carnival: The Historical Legacy*. Arts Council of England.

Brewer, J., Guelke, A., Hume, I., Moxon-Browne, E. & Wilford, R. (1996). *The Police Public Order and the State*. Basingstoke, Macmillan.

Brogden, M. & Shearing, C. (1993). *Policing for a New South Africa*. London, Routledge.

Bruce, S. (1985). No Pope of Rome: Militant Protestantism in Modern Scotland. Edinburgh, Mainstream.

Bryett, K. (1997). Does Drumcree '96 Tell Us Anything About the RUC? *Critical Criminology*, Vol 8 No 1.

B'Tselem (1992). *Limitations on the Right to Demonstrate and Protest in the Territories*. Jerusalem, B'Tselem.

CAJ (1996). *The Misrule of Law: A report on the policing of events during the summer of 1996 in Northern Ireland*. Belfast, CAJ.

CAJ (1997). *Policing the Police: A report on the policing of events during the summer of 1997 in Northern Ireland*. Belfast, CAJ.

Card, R. (1987). *Public Order: The New Law*. London, Butterworths.

Cawthra, G. (1993). *Policing South Africa: the SAP and the Transition from Apartheid*. London, Zed Books.

Cohen, A. (1993). *Masquerade Politics: Explorations in the Structure of urban Cultural Movements*. Oxford, Berg.

COMSA (1993). *Violence in South Africa: The report of the Commonwealth Observer Mission to South Africa*. Phase II: February 1993-May 1993. London, Commonwealth Secretariat.

Corso, G. (1979). *L'Ordine Pubblico*. Bologna, Il Mulino.

Cottrell, M. (1993). Green and Orange in Mid-Nineteenth Century Toronto: The Guy Fawkes' Day Episode of 1864. *Canadian Journal of Irish Studies* Vol.19. No.1.

Davis, S. (1986). *Parades and Power: Street Theatre in Nineteenth Century Philadelphia*. Philadephia, Temple University Press.

Della Porta, D. (1995). *Social Movements: Political Violence, and the State*. Cambridge, Cambridge University Press.

Donno, G-C. (ed.). (1990). *Storia e immagini del Primo Maggio*, Storiografia Italiana e Internazionale. Manduria.

Doolan, B. (1994). *Constitutional Law and Constitutional Rights in Ireland*. Dublin, Gill and Macmillan.

Estey, W.Z. (1996). *Report of the Commission of Inquiry into the Events of March 18, 1996 at Queens Park*. Ontario, Ministry of the Attorney General.

Fiore, C. (1980). *Ordine Pubblico*. Enciclopedia del Diritto, vol. XXX, Padova, GiuffrÈ.

Forde, M. (1987). *Constitutional Law of Ireland*. Cork and Dublin, Mercier Press.

Gora, J., Goldberger, D., Stern, G. & Halperin, A. (1991). *The Right To Protest: The Basic ACLU Guide to Free Expression*. Carbondale and Edwardsville, Southern Illinois University Press.

Hadden, T. & Donnelly, A. (1997). *The Legal Control of Marches in Northern Ireland*. Belfast, Community Relations Council.

Handelman, D. (1990). *Models and Mirrors*. Cambridge, Cambridge University Press.

Heymann, P. (1992). *Towards Peaceful Protest in South Africa: Testimony of multinational panel regarding lawful control of demonstrations in the Republic of South Africa*. Pretoria, HSRC Publishers.

Human Rights Watch/Helsinki (1997). *To Serve Without Favour: Policing, Human Rights and Accountability in Northern Ireland*. New York, Human Rights Watch.

Isnenghi, M. (ed.) (1996). *I luoghi della memoria*. Bari, Laterza.

Jackson, P. (1992). The Politics of the Street: A Geography of Caribana. *Political Geography* Vol.11 No. 2.

Jarman, N. (ed). (1997). *On the Edge: Community Perspectives on the Civil Disturbances in North Belfast, June - September 1996*. Belfast, Community Development Centre.

Jarman, N. & Bryan, D. (1996). *Parade and Protest: A Discussion of Parading Disputes in Northern Ireland*. Coleraine, Centre for the Study of Conflict, UUC.

Jarman, N. & Bryan, D. (1998). *From Riots to Rights: Nationalist Parades in the North of Ireland*. Coleraine, Centre for the Study of Conflict, UUC.

Jeffrey, A. (1991). *Riot Policing in Perspective*. Johannesburg, South African Institute for Race Relations.

Kaminer, R. (1996). *The Politics of Protest: the Israeli Peace Movement and the Palestinian Intifada*. Brighton, Sussex Academic Press.

Kealey, G. (1988). The Orange Order in Toronto: Religious Riot and the Working Class. In O'Driscoll, R. & Reynolds, L. (eds). *The Untold Story: The Irish in Canada*. Toronto, Celtic Arts of Canada.

Kelly, G. & Allen Nan, S. (1998). *Mediation In Practice*. Derry, Incore.

Kelly, J.M. (1980). *The Irish Constitution*. Dublin, Jurist Publishing.

Kelton, J. (1985). *The New York City St Patrick's Day Parade: Invention of Contention and Concensus. Drama Review*, Vol.29, No.3.

Knopff, R. & Morton, F.L. (1992). *Charter Politics*. Scarborough, Ontario. Nelson Canada.

Kretzmer, D. (1984). Demonstrations and the Law. *Israel Law Review*. Vol. 19, No. 4. LAW (1996). Annual Report of LAW: Human Rights Violations in Palestine. Jerusalem, LAW.

Long, M., Weil, P. & Braiban, G. (1984). *Les Grands Arrĺt de la Jurisprudence Administrative*. Sirey.

McCarthy, J. & McPhail, C. (forthcoming). The Institutionalisation of Protest in the USA. In Meyer, D. & Tarrow, S. (eds). *The Movement Society*. New York, Rowland and Littlefield.

MacPhail, C., Schweingruber, D. & McCarthy, J. (forthcoming). Policing Protest in the U.S.: 1960-1990. In della Porta, D. & Reiter, H. (eds). *The Policing of Protest in Contemporary Democracies*. Minnesota, University of Minnesota Press.

Mandel, M. (1994). *The Charter of Rights and the Legalisation of Politics in Canada*. Toronto, Thompson Educational Publications.

Mar'i, M. (1997). *The Right to Freedom of Assembly: An Analysis of the Position of the Palestinian National Authority*. Al Haq, Ramallah.

Marinelli, M. & Mazzei, A. (1988). *Temi e problemi della polizia: Orientamenti bibligrafici 1967-1987*. Brescia, Centro Nazionale di Studi e Ricerche sulla Polizia.

Marshall, T. F. *Community Disorder and Policing: Conflict Management in Action*. London, Whiting& Birch.

Marshall, W. S. (1996). *The Billy Boy's: A Concise History of Orangeism in Scotland*. Edinburgh, Mercat Press.

Mayekiso, M. (1996). *Township Politics: Civic Struggles for a New South Africa.* New York, Monthly Review Press.

Morange, J. (1997). *Droits de l'Homme et Libertès Publiques.* Paris, PUF.

North, P., Crilley, O. & Dunlop, J. (1997). *Independent Review of Parades and Marches.* Belfast: The Stationary Office.

Nunn, M. K. (1983). *Creative resistance: Anecdotes of Nonviolent Action by Israeli-based Groups.* Jerusalem, Alternative Information Center.

O'Rawe, M. & Moore, L. (1997). *Human Rights on Duty: Principles for better policing - International lesson for Northern Ireland.* Belfast, Committee on the Administration of Justice.

Pat Finucane Centre (1995). *One Day in August.* Derry, Pat Finucane Centre.

Pat Finucane Centre (1996). *In the Line of Fire: Derry July 1996.* Derry, Pat Finucane Centre.

Pontier, J-M. (1997). *Libertès Publiques.* Hachette Supèrieur, coll. les Fondamentaux, Paris.

Santosuosso, A. (1988). *I tuoi diritti.* Milano, Edizioni Hoepli.

Scoppola, P. (1995). 25 Aprile. Liberazione. Torino, Einaudi.

Shaw, M. (1997). South Africa's Other War: Understanding and Resolving Political Violence in KwaZulu-Natal (1985-) and the PWV (1990-). Unpublished PhD thesis. University of the Witswatersrand.

Shaw, M., Camerer, L., Mistry, D., Oppler, S. & Muntingh, L. (1997). *Policing the Transformation: Further Issues in South Africa's Crime Debate.* Halfway House, Institute for Security Studies.

Toner, P.M. (1989). The Home Rule League in Canada: Fortune, Fenians and Failure. *Canadian Journal of Irish Studies* Vol.15 No.1.

Townshend, C. (1993). *Making the Peace: Public Order and Public Security in Modern Britain.* Oxford, Oxford University Press.

Turpin, D. (1993). *Les Libertès Publiques,* Dunod, coll. Fiches Express, UniveristÈs, Paris.

van Koningsbruggen, P. (1997). Trinidad Carnival: The Quest for Identity. Warwick, Macmillan.

Waddington, P.A.J. (1994). *Liberty and Order: Public Order Policing in a Capital City.* London: UCL Press.

Wills, L. (1996). History. In *Images of the Carnival: The Official Lilt Notting Hill Carnival Book.* London: Creative & Commercial Communications Ltd.